ESCAPING NAZI ATROCITIES

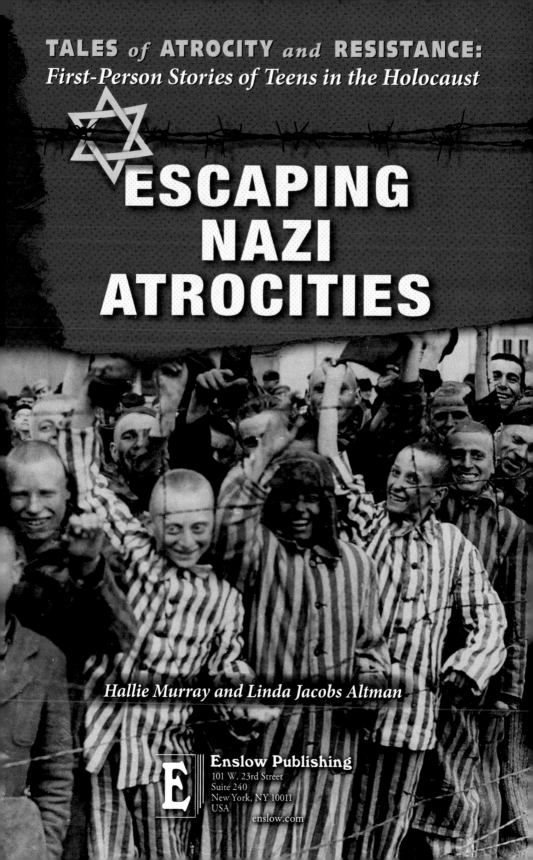

TALES *of* ATROCITY *and* RESISTANCE:
First-Person Stories of Teens in the Holocaust

ESCAPING NAZI ATROCITIES

Hallie Murray and Linda Jacobs Altman

Enslow Publishing
101 W. 23rd Street
Suite 240
New York, NY 10011
USA
enslow.com

*Special thanks to the people of the United States Holocaust Memorial Museum
in Washington, DC, for all their help in completing this book.*

Published in 2019 by Enslow Publishing, LLC.
101 W. 23rd Street, Suite 240, New York, NY 10011

Copyright © 2019 by Enslow Publishing, LLC.

Library of Congress Cataloging-in-Publication Data

Names: Murray, Hallie, author. | Altman, Linda Jacobs, author.
Title: Escaping Nazi atrocities / Hallie Murray, Linda Jacobs Altman.
Description: New York : Enslow Publishing, [2019] | Includes bibliographical references and index.
   | Audience: Grades 7–12.
Identifiers: LCCN 2018001407| ISBN 9780766098275 (library bound) | ISBN 9780766098282 (pbk.)
Subjects: LCSH: Holocaust, Jewish (1939-1945)—Personal narratives. | World War, 1939-1945—
   Refugees. | Teenagers—Europe—History—20th century. | World War, 1939-1945—Jews—
   Rescue. | World War, 1939-1945—Jewish resistance.
Classification: LCC D804.195 .M87 2018 | DDC 940.53/180922—dc23
LC record available at https://lccn.loc.gov/2018001407

Printed in the United States of America

To Our Readers: We have done our best to make sure all website addresses in this book were active
and appropriate when we went to press. However, the author and the publisher have no control over
and assume no liability for the material available on those websites or on any websites they may link
to. Any comments or suggestions can be sent by e-mail to customerservice@enslow.com.

Portions of this book appeared in *Escape—Teens on the Run: Primary Sources from the Holocaust* by
Linda Jacobs Altman.

Photo Credits: Cover, p. 3 United States Holocaust Memorial Museum, courtesy of National
Archives and Records Administration, College Park; pp. 6, 68 Keystone-France/Gamma-Keystone/
Getty Images; pp. 10–11 Corbis Historical/Getty Images; pp. 14, 26–27 Hulton Archive/Getty
Images; pp. 20–21 United States Holocaust Memorial Museum, courtesy of Charlene Schiff; pp.
32–33 Forum/Bridgeman Images; pp. 36–37 Rafal L/Shutterstock.com; p. 39 John Phillips/The
LIFE Picture Collection/Getty Images; pp. 44–45, 49 Fred Morley/Hulton Archive/Getty Images;
p. 54 Private Collection/Prismatic Pictures/Bridgeman Images; pp. 58–59 Bettmann/Getty Images;
pp. 64, 95, 100 Keystone/Hulton Archive/Getty Images; p. 72 Hulton Deutsch/Corbis Historical/
Getty Images; p. 78 Diamond Images/Getty Images; p. 86 Fototeca Storica Nazionale./Hulton
Archive/Getty Images; pp. 90–91 ART Collection/Alamy Stock Photo; p. 92 Hugo Jaeger/The LIFE
Picture Collection/Getty Images; p. 97 Universal History Archive/Universal Images Group/Getty
Images; pp. 104–105 Pacific Press/Sipa USA/Newscom; pp. 108–109 Imagno/Hulton Archive/Getty
Images; cover and interior pages graphic elements kikujungboy/Shutterstock.com (barbed wire),
ghenadie/Shutterstock.com (Star of David).

Contents

Introduction

There are many causes for and degrees of intolerance, but broadly speaking, racist beliefs usually result from fear and anger directed at a specific group of people who are somehow perceived as different or "other." Because of a psychological effect called "confirmation bias," people who are caught up in such fear and anger, or who learn racist ideology from their families or communities, tend to interpret news and events in a way that confirms their racist or xenophobic ideas. As these beliefs grow stronger, people start to do whatever they can to keep themselves "safe" by excluding others who don't seem to "belong" to their community. In movements like the white nationalist movement in contemporary America, this exclusion often escalates to violence.

Looking back, it can be difficult to understand why Jews and other persecuted groups didn't just leave Germany at the first sign of trouble. For some people, it wasn't financially possible, and others had nowhere to go. Still others stayed in Germany hoping things would somehow improve, and by the time it was clear that staying was more dangerous than fleeing, it was too late; anti-Semitism, like all other forms of bigotry, exists everywhere, even today, and they had no way of knowing that it might be safer elsewhere.

In what would become Nazi Germany, many people were incredibly afraid and angry about the German defeat in World War I. Adolf Hitler gained immense popularity through his charisma and his nationalist ideology. Though he had been involved in politics for a while, he rose to prominence when President Paul von Hindenburg named him chancellor, or head of state, in 1933. Hitler told the German people that they were a "master race," destined to rule the world. He also told them that Jews did not share this destiny. He said the Jews were a corrupt and vicious race, scheming for world domination. In Hitler's reasoning, Jewish Germans were not actually German, and they were actually intentionally hindering Germany's progress on the world stage. The obvious solution, according to Hitler and his supporters, was a progressive escalation of exclusionary anti-Semitic policies, which would eventually escalate to the full-scale violence and genocide of the Holocaust.

We don't know exactly how many people died in the Holocaust, but it is estimated that up to six million Jews were killed, along with millions of non-Jewish victims, including people with disabilities, Romani, political prisoners, gay people, and other civilians.[1] Others escaped with their lives, though the emotional trauma affected all. This book chronicles the stories of those who were able to somehow escape, whether that meant leaving Nazi-occupied territory in time, fleeing persecution on foot and relying on the kindness of strangers, or even hiding in plain sight among Gentiles. They experienced terrifying close calls and witnessed dreadful tragedies, but all, through some combination of chance and circumstance, managed to escape with their lives.

Chapter 1

Choosing When to Flee

Hitler was appointed chancellor of Germany in early 1933, and over the course of that year, the German government ceded more and more power to him and his party until a fascist regime had been established. Soon, Nazis controlled the entire German government and began enacting their anti-Semitic agenda. Step by step, Hitler and his Nazis transformed anti-Semitic ideas into anti-Semitic policies and actions in Germany. In April 1933, Hitler called for a one-day boycott of all Jewish shops. In May, crowds of young people burned hundreds of books written by Jews and anti-Nazis.

In 1934, all Jewish students were excluded from exams in medicine, dentistry, pharmacy, and law, and in 1935, one of the provisions of the Nuremberg Laws stripped Jews of their German citizenship. As German Jews lost their jobs, their property, and their civil rights, thousands decided to run while they still had the chance. They went to other European countries, to the Americas, to Asia—to any place that would take them. By 1938, about one-third of Germany's five hundred thousand Jews had left the

Schutzstaffel (SS) soldiers march during the 1933 Nuremberg Nazi Party rally. They are carrying banners with the swastika, which became a symbol of Nazism and German nationalism in the twentieth century.

The Nuremberg Laws

In September 1935 at the Nazi Party's annual rally in Nuremberg, Adolf Hitler called a special meeting of the German parliament, by then made up entirely of members of the Nazi Party, in order to pass two laws that together would later be known as the Nuremberg Laws. The first of these was the Reich Citizenship Law, which used racist Nazi pseudoscience to define which Germans were considered members of the Jewish race. It also decreed that Jews could no longer be Jewish citizens and stripped Jews and Mischlinge, or people who were considered half-Jewish and half-German, of many of their basic rights. The second was the Law for the Protection of German Blood and German Honor, which made marriage and any sexual relations between Jewish and non-Jewish Germans illegal. Situations that might lead to such sexual relations were termed "race defilement" because Nazis believed that such interactions would make the "German race" less pure.[1]

country. The two-thirds who remained clung to the hope that life would somehow get back to normal; they thought it would be riskier to attempt to flee the country than it would be to continue to live under Nazi policies. Yet, as we know now, the situation in Germany only went from bad to worse.

The Institutional Violence of Poverty

Because of Nazi policies, hundreds, then thousands, of German Jewish men lost their jobs or businesses. At that time, most women did not work outside the home. They ran the household and cared for the children. The task of earning a living fell to the men. When they could no longer perform this task, whole families plunged into desperate poverty.

Jewish men in these dire straits reacted in different ways. Liane Reif-Lehrer's father sank into depression after he lost his thriving dental practice. He eventually decided that the family would have to leave, regardless of the many hardships this would entail:

> So [my parents] went and applied for visas and passports and so on. On the morning of September 30, 1938, my father and mother actually left the house together to go pick up those passports. They picked up the passports and at about noontime, they parted to do separate chores. . . . I guess at about 2:30 in the afternoon . . . there was a phone call. My father had been found at the bottom of a staircase. I'm not sure whether he was already dead or whether he died either on the way to the hospital or right after he got to the hospital. But the death certificate says that he died of multiple fractures including a fractured skull and lots of fractured ribs. . . . [The] general consensus was that he had committed suicide. My mother didn't want anybody to know that and . . . I never, ever said anything until quite recently about that. . . . My brother's idea is that my father probably did commit suicide and that one of the reasons that he did it, aside from being depressed . . . was that he probably figured that a woman with two children would have a much better chance of escaping if there was no husband around. At that time, mostly it was the men who were being really harassed.[2]

13

Many Jewish storefronts were utterly destroyed in the violence of Kristallnacht. Here, a man cleans up glass from a broken front window.

After the Night of Broken Glass

The anti-Semitic violence of November 9–10, 1938, convinced many Jews that it was time to flee Germany. In Jewish neighborhoods, synagogues, homes, and businesses went up in flames. Shattered glass littered the sidewalks. This attack came to be known as Kristallnacht, the night of broken glass. According to Nazi propaganda, it was a spontaneous demonstration of outrage because a Jewish student had shot and killed a German embassy official in Paris.

Actually, the violence of Kristallnacht was not spontaneous at all. On November 10, 1938, a telegram from the SS (special security force) directed local officials to carry out violence against Jews. It further ordered mass arrests of "healthy male Jews, who are not too old."[3] In response to this order, thirty thousand Jews were arrested and sent to concentration camps.[4]

Fred Ederer's parents were making plans to escape Germany when the Nazis began their roundup:

> My parents . . . discussed a strategy for dealing with the Nazis, who, according to my parents, were sure to pay us a call . . . [and] would be looking for money and other valuables. My parents mainly expressed concern about the two bank books providing access to the funds we needed to booking passage to the United States. We expected to be able to emigrate in December, when our quota numbers for the American visas were due to come up. . . . My mother sewed into the back of the boys' pajama tops the two bankbooks—one bankbook into each pajama top. My brother and I went to bed early, as my parents hoped that the Nazis would neither disturb the children nor discover the bank books. My mother

15

prepared 30 marks in cash to turn over when they asked for money. My parents stayed up and waited.

They came at 11 o'clock, four of them—two SS-men . . . and two civilians. I was fully awake, but pretended to be asleep. They asked for money and my mother gave them the 30 marks. They then searched all the rooms, including the room my brother and I were in, and took all the jewelry and silverware they could find, which was essentially all of it. They did not disturb us children and did not find the bank books.

Finally before they left, I heard them ask my father to put on his coat—he was to go with them. . . . My father pleaded that he had never done anything wrong and that an Austrian colleague of his who had been a long-standing member of the Nazi party would vouch for him. . . . At long last, the men left—miraculously without my father.

The next day we learned that my father was the only adult male resident of the apartment house who had been spared; all the other men, about 20, had been taken away—to Dachau [a concentration camp]. . . . By the time we left . . . for the United States (January 19, 1939), the men had not returned. . . .

Kristallnacht was a clear signal to all the world that there were no limits to Nazi atrocities and served ample notice to Jews in Germany that there was no hope other than emigration—if only a safe haven could be found. Unfortunately, the few safe havens that existed were open to only a relatively small number of Jews.[5]

Difficult Choices

Considering the danger of living under German control, many have wondered why more Jews did not get out early.

Some stayed because they had no place to go or did not have enough money for the trip.

Some tried to get out, only to find that they had run out of time. Gerda Feldman was a teenager living in Germany when Kristallnacht tore her world apart. Looking back, she talked about why so many had waited too long:

> We had a grocery store. Once or twice my father was beaten up in the dark when he came home from the shop. And then things got a little difficult. But you see, when you're sort of 12, 13, you don't quite realize the dangers that were going on. . . . People always say to me, "Why did people not leave early on?," and the only theory I can have is, if you are very poor you can go because you've got nothing to lose, and if you were rich, you know at the beginning you were allowed to take your money out with you, but if you are a middle-class person then you sort of value a little bit of security.[6]

No Place to Go

Kristallnacht did represent a turning point, and many Jews took the riots as a sign that Germany was no longer a safe place for them and their families. After that night, thousands of desperate Jews clamored to get out of Germany, but in many ways it was already too late, as a large proportion found they had nowhere to go. Four months earlier, representatives from thirty-two countries had gathered in Evian, France. For nine days, they had discussed the plight of European Jews without deciding on any kind of unified policy. In the end, only the Dominican Republic agreed to open its borders to Jewish refugees. Other countries, including the United States, Great Britain, France, and Canada, feared that a flood of immigrants with no means of supporting themselves would become a drain on their economies.

While trapped Jews struggled to survive, Europe braced for war. It began on September 1, 1939, when Germany invaded Poland. The Polish army tried to mount a defense, but the German army overwhelmed them with a fierce assault that Hitler called *blitzkrieg* ("lightning war"). Poland fell in just three weeks. Under the terms of a secret pact with the Soviet Union, the Germans did not take all of Poland. They only occupied the western part of the country, up to the River Bug. The Soviets took the territory east of the river.

After the German invasion of Poland, in Nazi-occupied Warsaw, some young Jews wanted to get away from the Germans at all costs. According to fifteen-year-old Simha Rotem, these Jews

> organized in small groups, planning to go east, cross the River Bug, and get to the Russian-occupied zone. One of them was my cousin Simha . . . who was two or three years older than me. I wanted to go with him but my parents wouldn't let me, so I stayed. We got one mes- sage and then lost track of him. I don't know what became of him. I urged my parents, especially Father, to let me go to the Soviets, but to no avail. Once I did seem to convince Father, but the issue kept getting postponed. Meanwhile, refugees began returning from the Soviet zone bearing bad news, which didn't encourage moving there.[7]

Yitzhak Zuckerman worked in Warsaw with a Zionist youth group that prepared teenagers and young adults to settle in Palestine (present-day Israel). He never forgot the day that changed his life. When the war began

September 1, many cities were bombed, causing serious casualties, and everything was in an uproar. Yitzhak was in the village of Klebán at the time, having gone there for a conference. He raced back to Warsaw to discuss the situation with his colleagues in the movement: "By then we knew from the radio about the German advance. We figured that our Movement would retreat eastward, but it didn't occur to us that Poland wouldn't hold out at all, not even a few months."[8]

German Expansion

In the early twentieth century, Charles Darwin's theory of natural selection was being applied to areas, like government. One school of thought reasoned that if natural selection meant the most successful animals would survive and thrive, then the most successful nations would last the longest and grow the biggest. In Nazi Germany, *Lebensraum* was the term used for land that Germany needed to annex in order to expand and grow.[9] Just as the United States had expanded from the East Coast to the West and from the British Empire to a vast range of territories, the Nazi government thought Germany needed to expand into eastern Europe. After taking over countries across the continent, Nazis planned to deport all Jews and create a new space just for Aryan Germans to live. The first country Hitler invaded in an attempt to gain control of Lebensraum was Poland, which borders Germany to the east, though it wasn't the last by far.

Poland was only the beginning. One nation after another was crushed by Hitler's blitzkrieg: Denmark, Norway, Belgium, Luxembourg, the Netherlands, and France. With each new Nazi conquest, thousands of Jews fell under Hitler's control.

Shulamit Perlmutter (*right*) poses with friends before leaving for America.

Orphaned in Ukraine

Thirteen-year-old Shulamit Perlmutter (later, Charlene Schiff) lived in the Ukrainian town of Horochow, near the Polish border. The Germans did not get there until June 1941. As soon as they took control of the place, they set up

a ghetto for the Jews. This involved choosing a crumbling old neighborhood and forcing all Jews to live there. Shulamit lived in the ghetto with her mother and sister until 1942, when they heard rumors that the ghetto was about to be destroyed. Her mother began looking for a hiding place:

> [Mother] wanted to find a place where someone would hide the three of us. . . . One day, she came home and she was very excited, and she told us that she found two places. She couldn't find one place where the farmer or the people would be willing to hide three people, so she found two.
>
> One place would hide one person, and another place, the people were willing to take two people. And, there was my mother's difficult decision, how and who should go where. And in her infinite wisdom, she decided that my sister, being the older one, would be able to manage on her own, and mother and I would go to the other place, the two of us. . . . The plans were that [the farmer] would pick her up after work one evening, and that one morning when we all got up, we ate our meager breakfast, and my sister

21

took her little bundle with her, the most important things, clothing that she still had. She wasn't crying, and I wasn't crying either. We hugged, we embraced, and we said goodbye, and my mother kept saying how wonderful it would be when all this is over, we'll meet again, and papa will come home and we'll have great celebrations. And so, she and my sister went to work, and that evening my mother came back by herself, and she told me that my sister went off and everything was working according to her plan. . . .

A few days after my sister left, my mother came home from work and she says, "It's time to go." And so, she made me dress in my best clothes, and again, I still had that coat with a few sewn-in coins, and I put on my high-top shoes, and she got dressed . . . and made two little bundles, one for myself and one for her. We ate our meager supper, and when it got dark, really dark, . . . [we] walked out, we didn't say goodbye to anyone. And pretty soon we were in the river. . . . All of a sudden shots rang out, and we ducked . . . we just stayed there . . . the entire night. . . . The next morning, [we] . . . heard a lot of noise, a lot of commotion, we saw fire, we heard screams, we heard babies crying. . . . A lot of other people from the ghetto tried to do the very same thing we did, and they ran towards the river. . . . At that time, the guards started screaming, the Ukrainian guards. . . . "Crawl out, Jew, I can see you.". . . My mother held me down and we stayed put. . . . I don't know how many days we stayed in the river, but it was several days, and I kept dozing off. And one time I woke up, or I thought I woke up, and I looked around, and my mother wasn't there.[10]

Shulamit Perlmutter never saw her mother again. At the age of thirteen, Shulamit had become an orphan. She managed to survive by hiding in the forest near Horochow, scavenging for food, and keeping far away from other people.

The world became a place of horror for orphans like Shulamit. Some tried to run, some went into hiding, and some were too paralyzed by fear to do anything. All had one thing in common: the Holocaust had forced them out of a normal life and into a world gone mad.

Chapter 2

Traveling Through Hostile Territory

Escaping a dangerous situation is never the end of the journey; indeed, for many people, getting out of Germany was just the first step in a long, arduous road to a better life. As has been made abundantly clear from recent tragedies, including the Syrian refugee crisis, other countries are often reluctant to take in refugees, even those fleeing life-threatening situations. Governments believe, sometimes correctly and sometimes incorrectly, that taking in refugees will strain their resources and may cause issues on the international political stage.

As many Jews and other persecuted groups fled Germany, they often also had to travel through other countries under German control, as Nazis gained power across Europe. The search for refuge in countries under German control was both complicated and dangerous. Some used false identification papers, hoping they would not be caught. Others tried to find a country that would give them visas. Still, others slipped across international borders without papers. Regardless of what they did or where they went, young people quickly learned that uncertainty and fear were an inescapable part of their lives. They also learned that success or failure could turn on the most trivial of incidents.

The Flip of a Coin

In March 1939, teenager Ursula Bacon and her parents were waiting for a train that would take them out of Germany. Ursula noticed another family:

> A quietly dressed, middle-aged couple with two girls about twelve and fourteen years of age were standing amidst their four pieces of luggage at the edge of the crowd just outside the terminal. A couple of Hitler's brown-shirted SA men swaggered by, stopped at the little family which was most probably fleeing the country just as we were. The four people seemed to be shrinking into each other in a futile attempt to become invisible. One of the SA men made some remark that caused them both to break out in coarse, boisterous laughter. The other Nazi began twirling an iron crowbar expertly in the air, and with calculated accuracy suddenly brought it down hard on one of the family's . . . suitcases. The sharp points of the iron tool ripped a deep gash into the leather. In order to retrieve his weapon from the suitcase, the man yanked sharply, the rip widened, and with a death-knoll tinkling, several gold coins escaped from their hiding place between the leather and the lining. The gold pieces twinkled and danced on the marble floor for a brief moment, then came to rest at the . . . feet of the two Nazis.
>
> My father stood still as a rock, his eyes averted, glued to the floor. He was gritting his teeth so hard that I could hear a crunching sound. A strong muscle jumped

Nazi officers watch as Jewish families board trains to be deported from Germany.

on his right cheek, ready to burst through and attack the world. Mother's hand flew to her mouth as she stifled a soundless scream. Within seconds, shouting an endless barrage of Jew-swine-filthy-Jew curses and insults, the two burly Brownshirts herded the family on a fast trot out into the street and out of our sight, pulling the treacherous luggage behind them on a small cart. The mother, the father, and the two . . . girls would most probably not live to leave Germany.[1]

Ursula's family was luckier. The train took them to Genoa, Italy, where they made connections with a steamship bound for sanctuary in Shanghai, China. "WE MADE IT! We escaped!" Ursula wrote:

Father, Mother, and I made it out of Germany in the middle of a cold, fog-shrouded March night. Stealing out of town like thieves, leaving the scene of the crime of being Jewish. I shall never, ever forget those last few days we spent at home. Horror, fear, and panic closed in on us like an evil fog, sinister and unforgiving. Like the whirlpools of a gray and churning river it threatened to pull us down, swallow us, and leave no sign of us behind. I don't want to remember getting my father out of the Gestapo prison. I'm petrified that just thinking about it could bring it all back. But we made it; we did!

At last, we were on board our ship. There I was— tucked away in my little pocket of a cabin adjacent to the bigger one of my parents, about to sail on the steamship *Gneisenau*, on our way to China.[2]

Even in her joy, Ursula could not stop thinking about the family at the train station.

Brownshirts

The Sturmabteilung, or SA, was the militarized wing of the Nazi Party from 1921, when Adolf Hitler became the party's leader, to 1934, when it was replaced by the Schutzstaffel (the SS). The SA helped guard Nazi rallies and destroyed other parties by intimidating their members and fighting their paramilitary units. Members of the SA were often known as Brownshirts because of the color of their uniforms, as brown military uniforms were easily available after World War I. In the early 1930s, before the SS came to power, the Brownshirts represented one of the biggest direct threats to Jews, as they enacted a lot of the violence recommended or required by the Nazis in power at that time. Brownshirts were also known as stormtroopers, a name that probably inspired the evil Empire's stormtroopers in *Star Wars*.

The Trauma of Uncertainty

When the Nazis took over a town, they imprisoned or killed local government officials and any prominent Jews. They believed that taking away the leaders made the rest of the population easier to control. Leo Melamed's father faced special danger because he was both a Jew and a city councilman in Bialystok, Poland. When the Germans invaded, Mr. Melamed went into hiding with the rest of the council.

Leo kept a clear memory of that time:

My mother woke me in the middle of the night to tell me that I must get dressed; she's taking me to say goodbye to my father. The city was being bombed, and you could hear the air raid sirens and the "Aak aak" of anti-aircraft guns echoing through the buildings as we ran. My father embraced me, not knowing of course whether and when he was coming back and I of course knew nothing. And to leave us behind, not knowing what would happen, was the most difficult decision of his life.

[Later] my father called, and said that it was imperative for my mother and me to take the train out of Bialystok to Wilno [Vilna], that very night. My mother hurriedly packed a small suitcase with just enough for a few days, because that's all she thought we were going for. The train station [was] a madhouse. It was the last train out of Bialystok, and the whole family— my grandmothers and my aunt—came to the [train station] to say goodbye. But everyone knew it was just a temporary thing. This was until things straightened out and we would be right back. We never came back.[3]

Leo's father eventually caught up to his wife and son, and the reunited family began a long journey that would take them through the frozen wastelands of Siberia to a temporary safe haven in Japan. In 1941, the Melameds settled in the United States and made it their home.

Looking back on those years, Leo remembered the constant uncertainty:

You got used to the transitory life that you were leading and that there was no certainty. And you got used to that and it's part of being a refugee. It's a mentality that sets in. Everything is temporary. You don't know where you're going, where you're going to be. You may be here for a long time, you may be here for a short time. . . . [We] had no knowledge of the fact that we would be given permission to the United States or anywhere else.

We didn't know if we were going to stay in . . . Japan forever. We didn't know where else we would go. . . . [That's] the life of a refugee. The unknown becomes part of your keeping, part of your life.[4]

The family that remained in Poland did not survive: "[B]oth my grandmothers and my aunt—together with some 500 other Jews were crammed into . . . the [Bialystok synagogue]. The entire building was gasolined and torched, and they all died."[5]

The Eleventh Hour

Like the Melameds, many Jews had to leave family members behind. Some agonized over the decision, while others barely had time to think about it. Their lives depended on quick thinking and even quicker action. Eva Rappoport was not yet a teenager when her family made a hasty escape from the Nazis:

My parents decided we had to leave Vienna [Austria] and that our only chance was to go to France and it was really a last- minute decision and very hurriedly we decided to leave everything behind. . . . And I remember . . . my mother telling me that I was to go to my room and just pick the few toys that I wanted to take with me and be fast about it. . . . [I] started piling up . . . my things and my favorite dolls and mother . . . said, "Oh, no. You can't take all this," and she picked two dolls, and she said, "You can take two dolls. Period." And I was crying . . . [because] I thought it was terribly unfair to

Nazi soldiers stand in front of the wreckage of a burned synagogue in Bialystok, Poland. Hundreds of people, including members of Leo Melamed's family, were forced inside the synagogue, which was then doused in gasoline and set alight.

do this to me. . . . And so we . . . just threw some clothes in suitcases and . . . we went and said goodbye to my grandparents. . . . That was the last time that I . . . was [ever] to see them again.[6]

Tragedy and Tradition

Even people who decided to flee did not always realize the importance of getting out promptly. Edith Schleissner lived with her parents in Prague, Czechoslovakia. The first she had heard of Hitler was in March 1938, when Germany took over Austria: "When Austria fell . . . Mama, who had read *Mein Kampf* [Hitler's book] and believed every word, begged my father to flee to Paris, but he scoffed at her fears."[7]

In September 1938, Great Britain pressured Czechoslovakia to cede (give up) its Sudetenland region to Germany. Hitler assured Czechoslovakia and Britain that he was satisfied to have this strip of land on the German border.

Many Czechoslovakian Jews did not believe Hitler's assurances. The government started preparing for war and Jews started leaving Prague. Edith's father finally saw the danger and made plans to leave. He bought train tickets for March 10:

> Unexpectedly, [my grandfather] died on March 8, and his funeral was the next day. Mama wanted to leave as scheduled, but Papa insisted that the least he could do to show respect for his father was to sit Shiva [a Jewish mourning ritual] for the required eight days. It was an argument with which Mama could not disagree.[8]

The decision to stay turned out to be very poorly timed. On March 15, 1939, German troops occupied

Czechoslovakia. Edith remembered the dreary weather, and the radio announcer telling all children to go to school as usual:

> My parents, who had been so afraid of the event for as long as I could remember, acted as if nothing was different and hurried us out so that we wouldn't be late. But a lot was different. There were olive drab trucks parked all along the curb in front of my school. . . .
>
> Heavily armed soldiers stood at attention at either side of the entrance to the school, just like a pair of book-ends. A similar pair of book-ends stood inside the doorway. In the classroom pictures of Hitler glared at us from the top of each wall. What kind of army, I wondered, bothers lugging along so many pictures for school rooms, when, surely, they had more important things to do? I was also enraged that the Nazis felt they needed guns to protect themselves from little children. The morning was unusually subdued, and by the time we left to go home for lunch, my anger was all consuming. Without thinking of it, I stomped the foot of one of the book-ends and glared into his eyes. Much to my fury, he smiled at me benevolently and ruffled my hair.
>
> As I stepped out the door, Mama grabbed my arm and dragged me around the corner, away from the school. Then she squatted down to be at eye level with me. Shaking with obvious fear, she explained to me that what I had done was very dangerous and could have gotten me shot; that then I'd be dead and that she and the whole family couldn't bear that. She begged me, with tears in her eyes, to be good and to use self-control, to please, please stop asking questions and try to understand everything. Mama explained that there were things happening that were beyond anyone's

understanding. The fact that she didn't get angry with me and that she was pleading with me, made a deep impression. I promised her, and myself, I would do my best to comply.[9]

The city turned nightmarish, and the family knew it was time to leave:

Finally, early on the morning of April 9, we escaped from Prague. Papa had obtained permits allowing the whole family, Babi and Dzeida included, to go to the Tatra mountains [on the Polish-Czechoslovakian border] for Mama's recuperation [from pneumonia]. We were allowed to enter the railroad station, where we made our way to the Paris track. Papa timed it so that when we arrived, he had only enough time to waive the permits under the German guard's nose before the train started to move. We barely caught the last car of the train.

We crossed Germany uneventfully. At the border to France, ours was the last com- partment to be examined by both countries' border guards. Once again Papa waived the . . . permits under the German noses, and the French made them run off the train, as by then it was moving into France.[10]

The Schleissners arrived safely in Paris, but they would not be safe there for long because Germany invaded France in 1940. In their flight from the Nazis, they went to the Normandy coast of France, Spain, Portugal, and finally the United States.

The Ones Left Behind

For some, the decision to separate was more deliberate. Evelyn Konrad's father got visas for himself, his wife, and Evelyn, but not for Evelyn's grandmother. Other relatives tried to get her a visa, but without success.

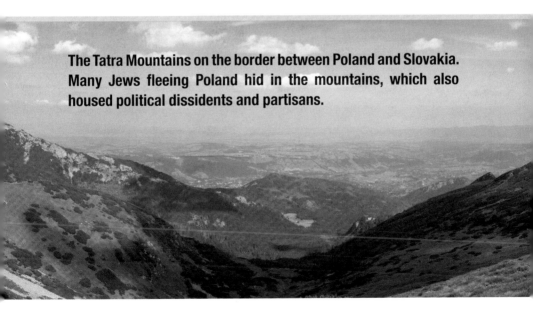

The Tatra Mountains on the border between Poland and Slovakia. Many Jews fleeing Poland hid in the mountains, which also housed political dissidents and partisans.

In time, the family had to face a hard truth; there was nothing to do but leave Evelyn's grandmother behind. Evelyn never forgot the day she and her mother went to say goodbye:

> We walked up the stone stairs to my [grandmother's] apartment. A skinny woman with feverish eyes, dressed all in black, opened up the door, face pale and drawn. She pointed to the front hallway and to my [grandmother's] bedroom, which was at the top of the long hallway. My mother thanked her, and the woman shrugged and walked back into another room, closing the door behind her. There were muffled sounds behind all the doors as we passed on the way to my [grandmother].
>
> "Who's there?" I heard her say behind her closed door in a strangled whisper, even though she knew that my mother and I were due that day.
>
> "Mutti," my mother said. The bedroom door was flung open, and my [grandmother] pulled us in, first me, and then my mother. Then she closed the door again and turned the key in the door.
>
> She looked less stout than she had been. Smothering me to her breast, she hugged me and kissed me and said, "Greterl, take the child out of here. Go back and take the first train. Please."[11]

Evelyn and her mother took the train to France, "but on the whole journey my mother sat in a corner crying, quietly, without a sound, and without stopping. I had never known that anyone could find tears for so many hours."[12] Evelyn's grandmother died on a transport to Treblinka, a Nazi death camp.

Members of Betar stand at the ready with a banner raised.

Poland, Palestine, Lithuania, Japan

In Volozhin, Poland, a Zionist youth group known as Betar was already operating when the Germans came. Zionists wanted to build a Jewish homeland in Palestine. Before the war started, going to Palestine was a "someday" dream.

During the war, many young Jews considered it a matter of life and death.

In 1940, sixteen-year-old Chaya Szepsenwol [now Lucille] and her older sister Feiga were members of Betar. Chaya remembered the night her sister came back from a Betar meeting with important news: "[The members] decided they were going to try to get to Vilna, and they thought well maybe from Vilna they would try to get to Israel. . . . [M]y mother thought [Feiga] was out of her mind. . . . But [Feiga] was . . . insistent and my mother realized that things were getting pretty rough."[13]

Once Chaya's mother had made up her mind, she did not look back. She helped pack two small suitcases and took the girls to the train station: "There were thousands, thousands of people trying to get on the train. My mother just pushed us on the train, and . . . sort of threw [our suitcases] after us [as] the train took off. We never got even a chance to say good-bye to her."[14]

The girls made it to Vilna, but nothing had come of the Betar's idea about going to Palestine. The two sisters were alone in a strange city, with no place to go. They managed to rent a furnished room while they considered the problem.

The solution to their problem came in the form of a rumor. A diplomat at the Japanese embassy in Kovno was handing out hundreds of exit visas for Japan. The girls decided to go to his office in Kovno to see if they could get one. They did not know that they were about to meet one of the heroes of the Holocaust, Chiune Sugihara. For twenty-nine days in July and August of 1940, he and his wife Yukiko wrote more than three hundred visas per day.

Chiune Sugihara

Chiune Sugihara (1900–1986) was a Japanese diplomat who issued visas to thousands of refugees fleeing Nazis in Lithuania. Sugihara was sent as a diplomat and intelligence gatherer to Lithuania in 1939 because he had become fluent in Russian during his time working in Manchuria, where he helped negotiate deals between Japan and the Soviet Union. As part of Japan's diplomatic efforts in Lithuania, he issued visas to members of the Polish underground so that they could escape Europe. When he realized how dire the situation in Germany and much of eastern Europe had become, he started issuing travel visas to refugees, even those who didn't have all of their paperwork in order. By the time he left Lithuania, he had issued over two thousand visas, allowing hundreds of refugees who might not otherwise have escaped safe passage through Japan to their final destinations in the Americas and elsewhere.[15]

Those visas that Sugihara gave out allowed thousands of Jews to find refuge in Japan.

In Kovno, long lines of desperate people circled the Japanese embassy. Chaya remembered standing in one of those lines:

> It was like about three or four o'clock in the afternoon and the office was closing at 5:00 or 5:30, and we saw that it was getting too close, that we would probably not be able to get in, so at one point where the door opened,

I grabbed my sister's hand and we just ran up the stairs and we tried to get in. And of course we tried to cross the line, so they pushed us down and we were right back on the bottom of the steps. We felt we were not going to make it that day. Finally we took courage again and we ran up those stairs, and I just put my foot right in the door, as they say, and was holding on to my sister, and we got in. We saw Mr. Sugihara. He asked us our name, he asked us where our parents were. We told him, my father was not living, my mother had no papers, and he looked very sympathetic at us and he just stamped, gave us the visa right there, on the spot. My sister and I got hysterical, we were just so happy, and there was a photographer walking around and he asked if we want to take our picture, so I have two pictures of my sister and myself on that day. August 12, 1940.[16]

Like other young refugees, Chaya and Feiga grew up quickly while they were on the run. They became clever and quick-witted, bold when they needed to be. Under ordinary circumstances, well-mannered Jewish teenagers did not barge into foreign embassies. However, circumstances during the Holocaust were very far from ordinary.

Chapter 3

The Kindertransport and the *St. Louis*

After Kristallnacht, many Jews became desperate to leave Germany. That terrible night they witnessed their synagogues being torched, their homes and businesses vandalized, and more than thirty thousand Jewish men imprisoned in Dachau and other Nazi concentration camps.[1] Most of these men were later released, but their freedom was only granted on the condition that they get out of Germany as soon as possible. At that point it had become nearly impossible for many Jewish families to leave the country, as Nazi actions had rendered many of them penniless. Those who found the money to leave often could not find a place to go, because other nations refused to accept so many refugees.

Some, however, were successful in their bids to exit the country thanks to a combination of sufficient resources, luck, and, in some cases, the aid of western European countries. The Kindertransport program and the voyage of the *St. Louis* were two famous rescue operations that allowed hundred of Jews to emigrate from Germany to Britain.

Children aboard the Kindertransport arrive in England from Germany in December 1938.

Commencement of the Kindertransport

In Britain, relief efforts were incapable of rescuing every refugee, so many relief organizations focused their efforts on saving the children of families stuck in Germany. These organizations set to work immediately after Kristallnacht, screening applicants, arranging transportation, and finding places for the children to live. An appeal for donations to pay for this expensive program quickly produced 550,000 pounds (over one million US dollars)—a fortune in 1939.

The program accepted children between the ages of six months and sixteen years. To pay for the individual living expenses, each child had to guarantee a bond of fifty pounds (about $1,500). Whenever possible, families posted this bond, but private donors came forward to help those who could not afford it.

The first transport left Germany by train on December 1, 1938, and arrived in England the next day, with two hundred children from a Jewish orphanage in Berlin. This first transport established a pattern that many others would follow. Children from small towns were taken to collection points in major cities, such as Berlin (Germany), Vienna (Austria), and Prague (Czechoslovakia). From there, they traveled by train to seaports in the Netherlands or Belgium, then by boat to the coast of England.

In England, volunteers sent each child to his or her temporary home. Some lived in private homes as members of the family. Others went to hostels, boarding schools, children's homes, or other facilities that could accommodate sizeable groups. Some teenagers were assigned to jobs as farm hands or household help. Neither the parents nor the children had any control over where and with whom the children would live.

Witnessing Countless Goodbyes

As one of the organizers of the Kindertransport program, Norbert Wollheim watched hundreds of families say their good-byes every day, many of them unaware that they would likely never see each other again. It was his job to keep everyone calm despite the heightened emotions in order the system moving. He kept an eye the timetables, reassured groups of anxious parents, and matched living children with names on a list.

In the course of these duties Wollheim saw hundreds of sad good-byes:

> [I]t was my function to see to it that these things were working properly. . . . [O]n a typical day we asked the parents to come with the children. . . . And there was a very special atmosphere in the air, expectation to a certain extent, there was laughing, and there were tears, and there was concern, and the last . . . advice by the mothers [about] what to do and what not to do, and . . . [when] the time of departure . . . came closer, and we had . . . reserved wagons which . . . had to be filled with these children. And . . . the police had insisted that the parents do not accompany the . . . children to the railways because there were certain difficulties. . . . They insisted that the goodbye had to be done . . . not in . . . public. So . . . when the time of departures came closer . . . I addressed the parents, and told them that the day of departure had come, and they should say goodbye because we're under strict order by the police . . . just to take the children up to the railways and they [the

parents] have to remain there. And . . . I [asked] for their cooperation and their understanding, because only that . . . would guarantee the continuity of our operations . . . then the parents said goodbye and again there was laughing and crying and a last hug. . . . Later [I often asked] myself the question, "How did I have the courage to say that to the parents?"

I only can answer that at this time we didn't know and we couldn't even foresee, we couldn't surmise for a moment that for many or most, it would be the last goodbye, that most of those children would never see their parents again.[1]

Saving Children, Separating Families

With so little information about what would happen when the trains arrived in Britain, parents who put their children into the Kindertransport program had to deal with uncertainty, grief, and some well-meaning people who second-guessed their decision. Alice Eberstarkova (Masters) was fourteen when her parents sent her and her two sisters to England:

[T]he fact that my parents agreed to send us will be a mystery for as long as I live . . . [E]verybody said to them, "How can you do that? How can you send your children away? Nothing is going to happen here." But my parents started to work very hard towards getting us out. That [meant] that my father had to spend an awful lot of money to get . . . the passports for the three of us. Then my mother started to sew and to accumulate clothes for three years ahead, all sized up to the ages of each of us for three years. . . . My father got the passports. My mother packed. We all had our suitcases. And one day they said, "You're going to visit [your uncle] in London."

Josepha Salmon, eight, arrives in England from Germany with her doll and a bag and little else.

. . . Then my older sister was the one who was made to take care of us . . . She was instructed very carefully . . . that she would be the acting mother; she was 15 . . . Had she been one month older, she wouldn't have been able to get on the transport because the transport only took . . . children from six months to 16 [years].[2]

Alice's parents tried to be matter-of-fact about the parting, but they did not entirely fool their daughters:

The morning that we were leaving we heard . . . my father cry for the first time. I've never heard my father cry. . . . We were all packed to go, and suddenly we heard this noise coming from another room. And we looked at each other in horror because my father was weeping . . . That's when we realized how awful it's going to be.

[When] we got to the [railroad] station . . . there were hundreds of people, parents and children, little babies. And we were put on a train. My mother couldn't decide whether to keep . . . my younger sister [age 10], so she put her on the train; she took her off. She put her on the train; she took her off again. And then she put her on the train at the last moment . . . Everyone was crying. The kids were crying. The parents were crying. The train pulled away, and we all waved goodbye and that was it.[3]

Alice and her sisters started their journey from Bratislava, Czechoslovakia, on a route that would take them through Germany:

[We] were very frightened when we came to Germany, because . . . there was an inspection.

The German uniformed soldiers came on the train . . . [and] they inspected our luggage. And we were frightened, and, of course, once we left Germany, we were all thrilled and cheered like crazy. . . . We were thrilled to be out of Germany and said, "Now we are— okay, we are safe."

And then we got on the boat.

When we boarded the boat, it was dark—it was night. And . . . people were sick, and they were given tea which was the worst thing I ever tasted in my life. It was English tea with milk in it . . . [T]here were matrons on the boat . . . I don't know who they were. Nurses. And we arrived. I don't remember much about the boat . . . I think we tried to sleep. I wish I could remember more about it.

The boat made port in Harwich, then a train took the children to Victoria Station in London. The Eberstarkova sisters were in the midst of what Alice called "an enormous commotion":

[W]e waited and waited for a long time, and finally our name was called, and there was our uncle picking us up. And he came with my guardian, because . . . he had to get a guardian for each of us . . . My guardian was Ms. Fannie Bandit . . . And she came . . . to meet us at the station, and my uncle said, "Now, we are going to drive to where you are going to live, in Burgess Hill. It's a children's home." And we were absolutely shocked about that because we thought we were going to stay with my uncle. I didn't know we were going to a children's home. And . . . I'm not sure, I don't know, well, of course, my uncle, it was weird. I understood why it happened, but my older sister was very upset with my uncle because she thought that he should take my little sister, who was 10 years old. But my uncle was in a very precarious position because he was just newly married, and he had a baby, and they had a small flat in London. And I think his wife was not inclined to take a child, although she says—and she was, she's very close to us now—I mean, we are very close. She says that, um, she participated, that she was the one who did most of the work to get us . . . out of Czechoslovakia. But she was not the sort of person who wanted to take a child in. I mean, she just, I don't know how that, how that happened. But in any case, the three of us went to this home in Sussex. It was called Wyberley . . . It was in beautiful grounds, a lovely place, lovely home. And they built sort of an addition to the back of this huge home where . . . the children were being housed. When we arrived, I, well, I can tell you now it was very painful that my uncle took us there.[4]

Alice and her sisters took comfort in letters from their parents, and sometimes packages of items their mother knitted, or fresh homemade cookies; things that were special because they came from home. The letters stopped abruptly in March 1942. Alice knew what that could mean. She was so frightened for her parents that she barely noticed the end of the war. Others could recall exactly where they were and what they were doing when they got the news. Alice could not:

I tried very hard to reconstruct that memory, but . . . I can't . . . I just don't remember exactly how I found out or where I was . . . But, of course, we immediately sent cables to Czechoslovakia to ask about our parents. And we had responses, lots of responses . . . because we sent cables to different people asking them to find . . . our parents.[5]

The answers to those cables confirmed Alice's worst fears. In June 1942, the Eberstarkovas were sent to Auschwitz and never heard from again.

Amnesia and Trauma

PTSD, or post-traumatic stress disorder, is a condition that develops in some people after they experience a traumatic event or series of events. Its major symptoms include having flashbacks or dreaming about the event, avoiding things that remind them of the trauma, depression, bursts of anger or fear, and an inability to fully remember details of the traumatic experience.[6] It was recognized as early as World War I, though back then it was called shell shock, and it was treated very differently.[7] The gaps in memory that some Holocaust victims, including Alice Eberstarkova and Inge Sachs experienced can often happen after suffering a traumatic event like separating from family at such a young age and under such difficult circumstances.

The Loneliness of Surviving

Like Alice Eberstarkova and many others, Inge Sachs had holes in her memory. She remembered parts of the long journey from Germany to England, but she did not have clear memories of leaving home:

> [B]eforehand I don't remember what I really thought about it. I thought it was a necessity. I was homesick, even then, before I left home. . . . Everybody was preparing to go, so it was nothing special that was just for me . . . I don't remember the night before [leaving]. My father took me to the railway station. I always understood that my mother didn't have the courage or the strength to take me, but I've read recently that only one . . . of the parents could take you to the railway station. . . . And

PTSD used to be called shell shock. This image shows a British soldier experiencing shell shock after the first World War.

we were sitting in the train, and I remember it was quite a cheerful occasion, actually. It was a sort of adventure. It wasn't cheerful at all for my parents. And then we left . . . They made us sing. And then we came to Hamburg, to the port. And there was [passport] control, and there were some women who . . . made a personal search . . . And then we came on board ship. . . .

I went to Southampton, but there was a stopover in France, in Avri, and we could go make a land excursion, and that was an adventure . . . I've never been outside Germany . . . and then the boat went on and landed in Southampton and from [there] we went by train. And in Southampton there was a number of ladies who gave each child a box with sweets and sandwich, and so on. And then we went to London, to Waterloo Station . . . And we sat on wooden benches, and the name was called . . . some youngsters went . . . to a boarding school. Some went to a Quaker organization, and many went to private people who wanted to take a Jewish child in. And I was one of those. [Then] my name was called and the name of the lady who was expecting me . . . So Mrs. Stevenson [my guardian] took hold of me, and . . . she drove me to her home . . . She was an elegant woman. I was lucky, she could speak some German.[8]

Inge had trouble adapting to her foster home. Though she never lacked for necessities, the foster home did not show warmth or friendly concerns:

I can tell you one thing that might illustrate [their] coldness . . . Everybody was going to leave the house, but the house couldn't be left alone. So it was decided that I should stay. So I stayed all [alone] over Christmas in the house. Snow was falling, to make it a picture. Well, when I learned that I couldn't leave, I couldn't go to my sister, to my relatives, I had the first nervous breakdown crying spell in my life. I couldn't stop myself. Afterwards when it came to the 21st–24th of December, I'd calmed down, but it was very, very hard.[9]

Like Inge Sachs, many of the Kindertransport children lived as strangers in a strange land; never comfortable in their temporary homes, never sure where they stood. They lived with secret grief and with memories they could never erase—but at least they lived. From its beginning in December 1938 to its end in September 1939, the Kindertransport program rescued ten thousand Jewish children from Germany and German-occupied countries.

Escaping to the Ocean: The Voyage of the *St. Louis*

In April 1939, when Jews were frantic to get out of Germany, the Hamburg-America shipping line announced that its luxury liner, *St. Louis*, would be making a special voyage to Havana, Cuba. Tickets quickly sold out. Of the 937 passengers, almost all of them were Jews fleeing the Nazi Reich. Most of the Jews had bought landing certificates and transit visas from Manuel Benitez, the director of the Cuban immigration office. The *St. Louis* left port from Hamburg, Germany, on May 13, 1939 and arrived at the Havana harbor on May 27. Gerda Blachmann (Wilchfort) was sixteen at the time, traveling with her parents: "We [came] to Havana. But we didn't really dock. We were out . . . far enough so we couldn't even see much of Havana. We just saw the silhouette of the buildings and of the harbor . . . and they told us to come to the dining room with the passports and the visas . . . to be admitted."[10] The

Cuban official who came aboard admitted twenty-nine passengers with valid documents and told the rest to wait until tomorrow.

According to Gerda Feldman, "We . . . were even told to get up very early the next morning and [we] had our breakfast and we lined up with all our suitcases ready to get off, and the boat stopped quite a way outside the harbor. Well, once again we thought that was quite normal, you know, it is [not] always deep enough for the boat to go right into the harbor."[11]

One tomorrow turned into another and then another, and still the passengers could not get straight answers to their questions. While they waited, American president Franklin D. Roosevelt tried to convince the Cuban government to admit the refugees. He could not bring them into the United States without violating the quota system of American immigration law. With Congress and the American people solidly against any such action, Roosevelt could not get the support he needed to accept the *St. Louis* refugees into the United States.

Returning to Europe

After a time, the passengers had to admit that their cause was hopeless. Gerda Blachmann remembered:

> [A] terrible mood . . . everybody was very depressed. Few people . . . tried to commit suicide . . . But you know, humans are always hopeful . . . [We] always cling to the hope something is going to happen. They're not going to let us rot on the ocean. I mean, something had to happen to us. Of course, the fear was that we would go back to Germany.

A group of Jewish refugees wave from the deck of the *St. Louis.*

Not Welcome Here

It is sometimes difficult to understand why a country would refuse to accept refugees like the Jews fleeing the Nazis. Wouldn't everyone want to help these people, who have already lost everything, find new homes? But accepting refugees is much more complicated than simply providing aid and space to individuals. A good contemporary example is the refugee crisis caused by the Syrian Civil War, which began in 2011. While the United States and other countries almost always accept refugees, there are so many people that have been displaced by the war and other factors that many countries of refuge feel overwhelmed. Citizens and governments of these countries start to fear that they don't have enough money or space to support everyone who wants to enter the country. In the United States, where many people hold unfair prejudices against Muslims, the fact that many Syrian refugees are Muslim is also scary. That fear can easily morph into something closer to hate or xenophobia, which is the irrational fear of foreigners, and people begin to try to restrict the number of refugees entering the country. It is important to remember in times of fear and hate that refugees have experienced terrible things in their home country, and that they aren't a threat at all. They just want to be safe.

[F]irst we came to the coast of Miami . . . I heard later that the captain had agreed that we make some kind of a forced landing or something but we didn't know anything about it. We just saw the . . . [United States] Coast Guard boats surround us near Miami to make sure that we wouldn't even come close . . . to shore, so that was out. So we saw the lights of Miami. We saw the lights of America and that was it. So we slowly sailed back to Europe.[12]

Nobody knew what would happen when they got back to Europe. Gerda Feldman called it a "grim atmosphere," and noted that

several . . . people tried to commit suicide and we had a group of young people checking all the cabins to watch people . . . [then] we heard that Belgium, Holland, France, and England were prepared to take a quarter each of the people . . . [A] lot of people wanted to go England, because the other countries were too near Germany . . . My father obviously knew what was going on because he sent us a telegram and said: "Choose England." But really one didn't have a choice. They decided where people should go and people's different nationalities . . . My mother told me to go and speak to the . . . English Immigration Officer because I had learned English at school. How good my English was I really don't know, but I did talk to the man and whether that had any influence or not I really don't know. But luckily we ended up in England.[13]

Ending up in England was very lucky indeed. Just a year after the _St. Louis_ returned to Europe, Germany conquered Belgium, Holland, and France, but not England. In England, one _St. Louis_ refugee died in an air raid. In the occupied nations, a total of 254 *St. Louis* refugees perished along with other Jewish victims.

Both the *St. Louis* passengers and the Kindertransport families took enormous risks to protect themselves and their families. They did what they had to do in spite of their fears and the odds against survival. With this courage, even those who did not survive defied their killers by taking back some control over their lives.

Chapter 4

Life on the Run

Once refugees had managed to escape Germany, they had to contend with the next dilemma: where to go? Travel was incredibly dangerous, as many were carrying false travel documents, or even no documents at all, and lived in fear of being found out. Even those with legitimate visas faced danger from Nazi-sympathizing officials and border agents. Anyone could be stopped, searched, and arrested at any time, and at national borders they could be delayed by immigration officers who might force them to return to Germany.

The Nazi blitzkrieg moved so quickly that many Jews had to keep moving in order to stay ahead of Nazi forces. In the spring of 1940, German troops overran Denmark, Norway, France, Luxembourg, Holland, and Belgium. Jews in those countries were forced to flee again and again as Hitler's influence expanded, always searching for the next safe space so that one day they might live without fear. Many were never able to reach that final place of refuge.

German soldiers raise the Nazi flag at a Belgian castle after the invasion of Belgium, signifying Germany's expanding influence.

The Safe House and the Surviving Son

When the Nazis invaded Belgium, Alfred Feldman and his family fled into southern France, making their way to the small town of Montagnac:

> On August 25 [1942] ... Mala Weiss passed on a warning from the local [police] that a *rafle* [roundup of Jews] was planned that night. My father, having obtained a certificate from the local doctor that he was too ill to work and still in possession of his release papers from the [work] camp, decided he could remain home. I, of course, had to be hidden. No one imagined that the roundup might include women.
>
> That evening, Mr. Granal [a neighbor] led me into their "cellar"; then up a ladder to the top of a story-high wooden wine vat, [then] over loose planks to the top of a concrete vat. There, among dusty discarded crates, he had arranged a hiding place for me. After remaining atop the vat for perhaps a week, it was not Mr. Granal but his wife who came up the ladder one day. She . . . looked distraught. She must have struggled long to get the terrible news off her chest . . . "They took your [mother]."[1]

Alfred and his father received a letter from Mrs. Feldman, saying that she was in a work camp (named Rivesaltes), along with Alfred's two sisters. Shortly after this, a refugee-aid organization found a place for Alfred:

> They told my father that I should come to Montpellier [a nearby town], where I would be given false identity papers and sent to a safe place . . .
>
> When I arrived in Montpellier, I left the bus stop quickly. "That is where they are watching," my father had warned me. "That is where they are checking

65

identifications." . . . My father had told me to walk unhesitatingly down the avenue and to hail a cab as soon as I saw one. He had given me the address of a safe house to which the cab was to take me. I was expected, he had assured me, and they would pay my fare.

I was lucky. I spotted a taxi almost immediately, and it stopped when I hailed it. But as I got in, a man followed me, pushed me over, and closed the door. Just another passenger trying to share a scarce cab, I thought. When the cabbie asked for our destinations, I, innocently, gave mine first. I realized the terrible mistake I had made as soon as the other passenger said, "That is where I go, too." He had been following me, I realized. He was no common passenger. He was an undercover policeman. And I was leading him to the safe house, betraying all inside.

As the cab rolled along, I risked a look at my pursuer. The man's eyes did not glint with the triumph of the sleuth cornering his quarry. They were downcast. He looked dispirited, as scared as I was. He must be a fellow refugee, I concluded, and we must have arrived on the same bus.[2]

That was only the beginning of Alfred Feldman's journey to survival. His mother and sisters were not so fortunate:

Convoy 31, the train on whose transport list the names of my mother and sisters appear, left Paris on September 11, 1942, carrying over a thousand deportees. . . .

Their train arrived in Auschwitz on September 13. Of its passengers, the German jailers selected some to work; the rest were gassed immediately. Among those selected for work were seventy-eight women identified by the numbers 19530 through 19607 tattooed on their forearms. None survived . . . I have not checked further . . . I have gone far enough.[3]

Hiding from the Death Squads

Alfred Feldman did not know the fate of his mother and sisters until much later in his life. But Sally Baran's (Eisner) thirteen-year-old brother actually saw the bodies of their parents. They became victims of the Einsatzgruppen. These were the killing squads that followed the regular German army into the Soviet Union. Sally's parents' lives ended in a trench they were forced to dig for themselves.

This happened in a Ukrainian labor camp, when Sally and her thirteen-year-old brother were working in the fields:

Einsatzgruppen

The Einsatzgruppen, also known as the death squads or the killing squads, were groups of German security officers whose job was to follow the German army as it advanced on the Soviet Union and all enemies of the Nazi Party behind German military lines, including Jews and political dissidents. Initially, they killed only men, but by 1941 they were tasked with killing everyone, including women and children. They would enter houses and community centers and systematically murder all residents.[4]

A member of an Einsatzgruppen unit prepares to shoot a Jewish man. The hole in the foreground is full of dead bodies.

It was in July 1943. We heard terrible sounds of shooting and shelling, coming from all over. We didn't know what was going on . . . I was in the fields working when the Nazis surrounded the camp grounds, ordered everyone, including my parents, to dig a mass grave—their own. Then they were ordered to strip naked and line up. Then they were shot, one by one.

When the firing stopped and the Nazis had left, my brother, who was thirteen at the time, went back from the fields to see what happened. He saw our parents lying, with all the others, in that large ditch that became their grave. He immediately ran away. I lay in the fields terrified until it became completely dark. I went back to the camp the very next day and saw the mass grave and pools of blood, all over . . . I started out in search of my brother. A day later, in a swampy part of the forest, I found him. We were both very frightened and utterly confused. He was practically speechless from shock.[5]

In their wanderings, Sally and her brother had many close calls. One of the closest happened when they were staying with a non-Jewish family, working for their room and board by helping with child care and farm chores:

One late afternoon, as dusk approached, my brother was chopping wood in front of the house and I was inside glancing out the window. I suddenly noticed three horsemen approaching. Someone had obviously told the Ukrainian police about our presence and now they were looking for us . . .

I ran outside, grabbed my brother's hand pulled him inside and pushed him and myself under the . . . bed . . . to hide among the boots, shoes, and many other items that were stored there. We crept as far into the corner as we could, pressing our bodies against the wall . . .

We heard the loud bang as they pushed open the door . . . They started to search the house . . . They thrust . . . bayonets under the bed, sweeping the floor with the blades, stabbing and jabbing into the dark and cluttered space, pulling out boots and shoes. I felt the knife point against my skin but we didn't make a sound. . . . When they were convinced that no one was under the bed, they went outside . . .

We stayed under the bed for a long time after, afraid to come out. When the family came home and we told them what happened, they . . . told us to leave. It was a bitter cold winter night. We wandered about for days and finally ended up in a labour camp.[6]

Split-Second Decisions

In Germany and Nazi-occupied territory, survival could depend on snap decisions and timely hunches. This was the case for teenager Florence Gittelman and her father:

[It was] just the two of us . . . [Father] . . . spoke fluently Russian, and he had a profession. So he used to knock at the peasant door and said if they need a haircut, or a shave. And he said he has to clean up his daughter. So one family—I remember just like today, a nice peasant family—they took me in. They gave me a bath. She said, "I have nothing to wear for you" . . . But she went into the pig house—they . . . raised pigs—and they took off the blankets from a pig and she wrapped me around. And she gave me a little kerchief to put on my head, and she says, "Look, I would love to help you, but I can't. You have to leave the house immediately." But I cleaned up . . . and they killed the lice from this little outfit I wore. And we had to leave, so we left . . . and this is what we did for quite a few months. Walking at night— walking daytime, sleeping in the woods . . . and looking for the underground people [Jewish freedom fighters in hiding]. Where are the underground people? . . . [Father] knew if there [were] a lot of us, somebody was going to tell on us from the peasants; they gonna get us. Sure enough, we joined some Jewish groups, and we went into this house, and my father said . . . "You know, . . . we have too many people. Let's get out of here." And he grabbed me and we left, we left this way. From [the other side] the Germans were already there. They killed everybody [in the hideout].[7]

Toward Safety in Sweden

Margrit Rosenberg (Stenge) and her parents fled to Norway when Hitler took over in Germany. They were safe enough there until Germany conquered the country in 1940 and, all too soon, began deporting Norwegian Jews to concentration camps. Margrit was only thirteen at the time, but she could still sense the fear and tension present in her home. Einar Wellen, a member of the Norwegian underground, had promised to get the family out of the country, but the deportations continued and Wellen did not come:

> We had almost given up hope, when in the early morning hours of January 14, 1943 there was a knock on the door. Fearing the worst I opened the door. Relief surged through me when I recognized Einar Wellen with another young man, who turned out to be his friend Arne Myhrvold. Both were exhausted and frozen, because they had spent the night traveling, the last part on an open truck bed. The two young men wasted no time in telling us that everything was arranged for our

Children line up outside a labor camp in Poland. Even the youngest were given difficult work to keep them busy.

escape and that we would be leaving early the following morning. They advised us how to dress and what to bring in our knapsacks. . . . We would travel by truck to a small place near Fagernes, where we would board a train headed for Oslo [Norway]. We would leave the train in a suburb of Oslo. A minister, recognizable by his clerical collar would meet us at the station and take us to his home where we would stay until the next transport to Sweden [a neutral country].

This plan sounded easy enough, but we all knew that danger would be lurking in every corner. The truck could easily be stopped for an inspection, and what was even more likely was, that we would be asked for identification papers on the train, but these were risks we had to take to save our lives. . . .

We left Rogne at dawn the following day. Our truck made it without incident in time for the train to Oslo. Einar and Arne traveled on the same train as we, but in a different compartment, and in fact we did not see them again. My father hid behind a newspaper, my mother and I tried to look as relaxed as possible. Not one word was spoken between us. By some miracle we were not asked for identification papers. When we reached the suburb of Oslo, where we were to meet the minister, we got off the train and looked anxiously around. But he was there, a car drove up immediately, and we were off to the minister's home…[8]

The next stop was a barn, where the Rosenbergs joined a group of other runaways. All of them boarded a truck for a two-hour drive that took them close to the Swedish border:

Scandinavia in World War II

Denmark, Norway, and Sweden were all targets of German expansion in World War II because they were strategically located close to the Soviet Union. All three countries attempted to remain neutral, but only Sweden truly succeeded. Early on in the war effort, in 1939, Denmark, the closest to Germany of the three countries, signed a nonaggression pact in the hopes that it would prevent Germany from mounting a full invasion. Yet German forces still occupied the country, using it as a stepping stone to Norway. Norway was also a good strategic location for the British army, so both Britain and Germany occupied the country during war, while the exiled Norwegian government fled to London. The Nazi government made serious attempts to create a fascist Nazi state in Norway but failed to take over completely, and a resistance movement arose that worked with Britain to bring down the Nazis in power in Norway. Only Sweden remained truly neutral, allowing both Nazi soldiers and Allies to pass through unharmed. As such, Sweden also became an appealing refuge for the many political dissidents and Jews who had fled other Nazi-occupied nations.

[We] were told that this was the end of our drive and that we would have to walk the rest of the way to the Swedish border. A guide would accompany us.

We walked through the snowy woods, quickly and in absolute silence. Suddenly a small cabin appeared as if from nowhere with lights blinking through its windows. And then we heard: "Welcome to Sweden, come inside," and saw the outlines of two Swedish soldiers coming towards us.

Our long odyssey, beginning in Oslo on April 9, 1940 had ended.[9]

It was autumn 1945, and the Rosenbergs were finally safe.

Lady Liberty

Twelve-year-old Evelyn Konrad and her family found refuge in France until the French government declared all people from Germany and Austria "enemy aliens." It did not matter that Evelyn and her parents were Jewish, and therefore stripped of citizenship in their native land; they were Austrians who spoke German as their primary language. In wartime France, that was reason enough for leaving: "By February 1940, my parents were desperate to get out of France. Every day there were more news items in the papers about internment of enemy aliens. All of us were frightened by the . . . frequent air raids. Finally, my father got us a one-month visitors' visa to Portugal."[10]

They ended up staying in Lisbon, Portugal, for three months. That ended abruptly one night:

[M]y father picked me up out of my bed while I was asleep, and carried me to a car that took us to the pier.

There, I heard my mother say, in terror, "That small a ship?" and heard my father say, "No, that one." I sneaked a peek, and next to the small ship I had seen my mother point to, I saw a tiny little ship. "But it's smaller than the little [boat] that runs up and down the Seine and never leaves Paris," she said. I squeezed my eyes shut, hearing all the good-byes between my parents and my Uncle Freddie, and I fell asleep again. . . .

I'm not sure whether it was the sun through the porthole or my mother's moaning that woke me up. On the bunk bed across from me in the cabin, I saw my mother writhe and heard her moan and beg to die. Her cheeks had lost their rosy color; they were all sunken and grayish-white. The door to the cabin opened, and my father staggered in, moving like someone who had had too much to drink.

"What's wrong?" I asked, jumping down from my bunk bed.

"Don't you feel it?" my father asked. I shook my head. "Thank God," he said. . . .

The very first day out of the Azores [islands], it was pouring rain. In the morning when I woke up, my tummy felt as if I had left it behind in Santa Maria. I felt like throwing up, but I have never been able to throw up, and all that awful feeling stayed inside of me.

At night I did not sleep well, not because I was seasick, but because I was desperately worried about the German U-boats [submarines], that we had read so much about. . . . They were said to control the Atlantic, and no ship could escape them. So, during the day, I would go up on the deck and look out at the gray, rough ocean, searching for periscopes, so that I could warn the captain. . . . The only thing that reassured me about our ocean crossing was that we were carrying cork, and

This image of the Statue of Liberty in New York Harbor was taken in 1940.

cork floats. I was a very strong swimmer and thought that if our boat was torpedoed, I would swim to one of the floating stacks of cork. I would pull my mother and father up with me, and we would float until we got to land or to a convoy from America . . .

After nearly two weeks of seeing nothing but the gray sea . . . we came into a quiet zone of calm ocean, wrapped in a thick, thick fog. It seemed to me that [the boat] did not move at all. Every hour or so, she let out the mournful sound of her fog horn. I thought we were sitting ducks for the U-boats, and I prayed more often and more multi-lingually than ever before.

At the end of the second day, the fog lifted, and in the distance, but clearly visible, was New York harbor, with even the Statue of Liberty showing.[11]

Escapes to East Asia

In Kaunas, Lithuania, Hanni Sondheimer had to get visas for her family's escape:

When my father sent me to get the visas, I was a nervous wreck, and I was very angry, and he said, "You must, I can't lose one day's work because I'm lucky [to have a job]." It was awful. I must have stood there for many days. . . . When we were close to leaving my mother got sick and she had a fever and the doctor came to the house and gave her a prescription.

She . . . said they couldn't go, and we forced her to go, we said, "We don't care. Whatever it takes." She had to come with us. . . . On the ship to Japan we slept like on top of each other, close, because the ship was very full.[12]

The family did not have to worry about Nazis in Asia, but they did face hardship: "In [1943] . . . we were put into a ghetto [in Japanese-occupied Shanghai, China]. We had no toilets; we built our own toilet on a roof garden, and every morning they'd empty the pot, take it downstairs in the alley and clean it, put the stuff in a little wagon, it was bad."[13]

In 1940, eighteen-year-old Ruth Berkowicz and her father made their way from Vilna, Lithuania, to Japan, and from there were sent to Japanese-occupied Shanghai, China, by an even more complicated route:

Well, when the first people started going across to . . . Japan . . . we applied for an exit visa. You . . . not only

79

[needed] a transit visa to Japan—you know the transit visa was only for ten days—but . . . also had to get an exit visa from the Soviets. And so . . . we applied for exit. . . . There was a room . . . where the man . . . read a list of people who were getting exit visas that day. And one day . . . they mentioned my name, without my father. So I got very upset. I didn't want to go by myself across the Soviet Union and leave my father behind . . . It was no good. And so . . . I came home and I said to my father, "They read my name. They didn't read your name." And my father said, " . . . Ruthka, you have to go. You are 18 years old. You are young. You have your whole life ahead of you. You've got to go." And so I decided to go. . . . Two weeks later my father came.[14]

The Kindness of Strangers

Even in the desperate times of the Holocaust, fugitives occasionally received kindness from others. Ten-year-old Johanna Gerechter and her parents found a safe haven in Italy, although it supported Germany in the war. The Gerechters left Germany with ten marks per person. By the time they arrived in Bologna, Italy, they had used all their money:

> [We] stood on the platform in Bologna and really didn't know where to turn. To our great surprise . . . there were Italian students who . . . were organized by the Jewish community of Italy. . . . [T]hese students had made it their business to be there and . . . receive German or other immigrants that were fleeing Germany. Well, I remember two students taking us in hand, taking us to a beautiful, beautiful hotel, and caring for us for an entire week until we were able to receive money from our relatives in America.[15]

Some Jews found help from complete strangers. The quick thinking of a woman that Erika Eckstut had never met rescued her from the clutches of a German soldier. It happened when Erika was posing as a Gentile in order to buy food outside the ghetto:

I saw a German soldier beating a man on the ground who was bleeding. The soldier was on crutches and his chest was full of decorations. He stood on one of the crutches and with the other he beat the man. I approached the soldier and in my perfect German lectured him on how wrong he was to beat a man who did not defend himself. As I was busy giving my lecture, people stood around listening. All of a sudden a policeman touched my arm and said, "That will be enough little girl; let's go home."

At that moment I realized, "I can't go home. If I take him to the ghetto my whole family will be killed." So I took him to an opera singer who lived not far from the ghetto. She was, of course, a gentile. When we arrived at the door and rang the bell a beautiful lady opened the door and I said, "Mama." The policeman at the same time said, "Is this your daughter, Madame?" She ignored him, and pointing a finger at me, she said: "I told you once, I told you twice, home and homework." The policeman in the meantime kept repeating his question, and, in desperation, she started hitting me in the face. It was so painful that I hardly cared what happened at this point. Then, as if in a dream, I heard the policeman saying, "Keep her, keep her, just stop hitting her." After the policeman left, she took me inside, gave me a hug, and asked, "Are you from the ghetto?"

I have forgotten so many names from during the Holocaust, but I still remember her.[16]

In a similar incident, Roza Weintraub's father saved a fellow Jew he happened to see on the train:

Since [Roza's father] went by train a lot, he knew all the officials. He saw this refugee standing in the door, without hope. He could see that the man was a Jew, [and] he said: "What's the problem?" The man said: "I have only one option left—to jump off the train." He came from Danzig, and wanted to reach Vilna. His family was in Vilna. He had earlier been caught and sent back to Germany. So father bumped him, hugged him, started to kiss him and said: "Oh, it's good to see you, my brother, I am very happy to see you." Father took some money from his pocket, put some Lits [Lithuanian currency] into this Gendarme's pocket, and rescued the Jew. Later there was a recurrent thought. When I was in Russia and people were nice to me, I said that's because of father, because he had helped the refugees a lot. That's the thing I had to go back for.[17]

These spontaneous rescues took courage, daring, and an ability to think fast in dangerous situations. Though these rescues did occur, they were not common; the Nazis had seen to that. In the occupied nations, the penalty for helping Jews was death. Even well-meaning people were often too afraid to help.

Jewish fugitives learned to live with this. They became wary of strangers and were careful not to reveal too much about themselves. Many made a point of not staying too long in any one place. They lived in constant fear of recognition and capture. Many fugitives who eventually found sanctuary faced a new challenge: learning to live as strangers in an unknown land, surrounded by cultures they did not understand. For young people who missed their homes and families, adjusting to this life was an act of courage.

Chapter 5

Alicia's Journey

Alicia Jurman was born in Poland in 1930, the second-youngest of her siblings, all boys except for her. In 1941, when she was eleven years old, Germany invaded eastern Poland, and Alicia's life was changed forever. In the Polish city of Buczacz, Jews watched in horror as the Nazis came into town. Years later, one image stuck in Alicia's mind: "Mostly I remember the motorcycles. To this day I shudder when I hear the roaring sound of a motorcycle outside my house. No one really knew what would happen, and everyone was in shock."[1]

Endless Thunder

In a matter of days, the Germans called for Jewish men between the ages of eighteen and fifty to register at the police station. Alicia's father reported as ordered, expecting to be home by lunchtime. Around two o'clock, the family heard a distant noise. It rumbled, it cracked, it stopped and started throughout the afternoon. *Thunder*, Alicia thought. It had to be thunder.

After three days with no word, Alicia's brother Zachary remembered that odd noise: maybe it was not thunder at all. Maybe it was something much worse than thunder. When Alicia realized what her brother meant, she flew into a wild rage. "It *was* thunder!" she screamed, and set out to prove her point: "I ran over the [meadow] and into the woods. I went back and forth, calling and calling. 'Papa! It's Alicia! Papa, where are you?'"

Exhausted and grief-stricken, Alicia faced the truth; her father would not be coming back. He was gone, and so was the life she had known. Years later, writing about her experiences, she chronicled the destruction of her family:

> First they killed my brother Moshe. . . .
> Then they killed my father. . . .
> Then they killed my brother Bunio. . . .
> Then they killed my brother Zachary. . . .
> Then they killed my last brother, Herzl.

Three Narrow Escapes

In the months to come, Alicia would fall into enemy hands three times. The first time, she ended up in a sealed boxcar on the way to a Nazi death camp. She escaped because two men loosened the steel bars from a small window, and began pushing children off the train.

When Alicia jumped out, a bush broke her fall, leaving her bruised and scratched but otherwise intact. She watched as the train with its human cargo crested the grade and disappeared from sight. Then she did the only thing she could think to do: followed the railroad tracks back home.

In December 1942, Alicia was picked up again and sent to a notorious prison near the town of Chortkov, where she was beaten senseless and left for dead. A Jewish burial detail literally snatched her from the grave and took her to a kindly Jewish couple who nursed her back to health.

Alicia returned to Buczacz only to be caught up in the final liquidation of the ghetto. To make the city *Judenrein*, or free of Jews, the Nazis sent some to death camps and others to a ghetto in the town of Kopechince. At first, the Jurman family considered themselves very fortunate to be chosen for the ghetto. Then an *Einsatzgruppe*, or death squad, swept into town. Alicia managed to hide her mother and little brother, but she could not hide herself. Along with other Jews from the ghetto, she was marched to a field outside of town. The first thing she noticed was a freshly-dug trench making an ugly brown scar on the land:

> There were many Jews at the trench already, some undressed and some still undressing. Then the shooting started. We were pushed from the back by the barrels of machine guns and, as we approached the trench, we were confronted by more machine guns. Some people in front fell into the trench dead, and some still alive. . . . [A]s I was nearing the pit, I thought I heard my name being called.[2]

The next thing Alicia heard was machine gun fire, coming from a new direction. Then there was a voice, shouting her name: "Alicia, run! Get out of here! Run!"

Both the voice and the machine gun belonged to a friend from Buczacz. Alicia ran, hard and fast, across the meadow and into the woods beyond. She ran until her legs trembled and her breath came in heavy, painful gasps. Then she collapsed on the ground and cried.

This map shows where the concentration and death camps were located in and around Poland. It was created by the Allied forces after they liberated the camps following World War II.

86

Working to Survive

Alone in a strange part of the country, Alicia had no idea how to get home. She did know one thing, though: if her mother and brother were still alive, she would find them in Buczacz. In the meantime, she needed food. She made her way to farm country, hoping to find work in the fields.

On her first day, she helped to weed a potato field, for which she received a cup of sour milk and a small piece of bread. The next day she moved on to another farm, then another, and yet another. She worked hard and said as little as possible about her personal life. Alicia finally made her way to Buczacz and found her mother, but not her little brother. He had disappeared from Kopechince, and had not been found. Mother and daughter had to go on alone. They left Buczacz as quickly as possible, taking back roads through farm country. Mrs. Jurman was too weak to work in the fields, and, in any case, could easily be spotted as a Jew. She hid during the day, while Alicia worked at surrounding farms.

Some of the farms where Alicia worked belonged to Poles and others to Ukrainians. At the time, Ukrainians and Poles did not get along well due to a history of tension and violence, so Alicia crafted two identities for herself: "Helka" for the Poles, and "Slavka" for the Ukrainians:

> I had to be careful approaching the farmers to ask for work; what if I addressed one in Ukrainian and he turned out to be Polish? He would certainly turn me away, and then I would have lost the chance to work and get a piece of bread for my mother. On the other hand, if I spoke Polish to a Ukrainian, something even worse could happen—the man might come after me

From Enemy to Ally and Back Again

During World War I, the Soviet Union was part of the Allied forces and fought against German forces along with the United States, Britain, and France. Twenty-one years after World War I had ended, however, in August 1939, Joseph Stalin and Adolf Hitler signed a nonaggression pact between their two countries, the Soviet Union and Germany. The secret agreement also contained plans to split up eastern Europe between the two nations after toppling the governments currently in power in places like Poland and Lithuania. One month later, both the Soviet Union and Germany invaded Poland, which they split between them. Less than two years later, however, the pact between the countries was dissolved when Hitler invaded one of the territories that was meant to belong to the Soviet Union. Following this betrayal, the Soviet Union and German fought bitterly. By the end of World War II, the Soviet Union was firmly set against the Nazis, and Soviet soldiers led the liberation of many concentration camps, including the liberation of Auschwitz in 1945.

with his shovel. So the first moment that I approached the farmers was always crucial. On my way across the field I always tried to swing close to other workers and listen to their conversation to find out what language to use. If I had no choice and had to approach the farmer directly, I mumbled my greeting and waited to find out in what language he would answer.[3]

Along the way, Alicia made friends with an elderly Pole whose epileptic seizures made him an outcast. Superstitious neighbors thought he was possessed by a demon. In time, his tiny cottage became a safe haven for the Jurmans and other Jewish families. With a safe place for her mother, Alicia could wander as far as necessary to find work.

Soviet Rescuers

March 24, 1944, was a day Alicia would never forget. Soviet troops liberated the area they were living in, forcing the Germans into full retreat. Alicia and her mother made their way back to Buczacz, not quite knowing what to do. In this way, they were not alone:

> Everyone—and by that I mean about two hundred and fifty Jewish survivors—was in a daze, filled with a terrible feeling of loss and pain. I remember waking up several times each night during those first days because the bed was actually shaking with my mother's silent, convulsive sobbing. I knew that she waited until after I was asleep to release her grief and longing for my father and my brothers, and so I pretended to be asleep each time this happened.[4]

After two months of freedom, Alicia and her mother, along with the other Jews of Buczacz, were beginning to think about rebuilding their lives. Then the unthinkable

Gruß aus Buczacz.

Pozdrowienie z Buczacza.

An old postcard shows a street in Buczacz, a Polish city that was liberated by Soviet troops.

happened: the Nazis came back. When their artillery bombarded the city, Mrs. Jurman got hit by a piece of shrapnel and lost a great deal of blood. Alicia managed to get her mother back to their apartment, but there would be no running this time.

Mrs. Jurman had other ideas: "You must go, Alicia. . . . You must survive. You are the only witness to what happened to our family, to our people."[5]

Alicia could not bring herself to leave, and so mother and daughter waited. They hoped for the best, but they were not surprised when SS men kicked in the door and ordered them into the street:

> As we stood there shivering, clinging to each other, one of the SS men stepped back, drew his pistol, and aimed it right at me . . .

> What happened next only added to the nightmare. I heard the gun go off, and suddenly my mother lay dead at my feet. She had thrown herself between me and my murderer and had been hit by the bullet meant for me.[6]

The SS man pointed his gun at Alicia and pulled the trigger, but nothing happened. He tried again, but still nothing. He was out of ammunition: "I will never know why he did not reload or why the other SS man did not shoot me, but for some reason they decided to take me to prison instead."

Once more, Alicia was marched to a killing field—the very meadow where the SS had killed her father. A fresh trench waited to be filled with bodies. Alicia positioned herself at one end of the line and, at the first opportunity, made a run for the woods.

So the running began again, and Alicia had no idea when it might end. Part of her wanted to give up—sit down somewhere and quit struggling. But she remembered what her mother had said about surviving, so she kept going. It was the only thing she could think to do.

Telling the Story

Alicia survived the war, but she did not stop moving. At a time when Palestine had immigration quotas, she smuggled

SS officer Kurt Daluege gives the Nazi salute, while Nazi politician Adolf Wagner stands in the background in Munich in 1938.

Holocaust survivors into Israel. She went to Israel, but she did not stay. She met and married Gabriel Appleman, an American Jew, and went with him to the United States. There, she could finally start building a new life.

She wrote of her experiences in an autobiography, published in 1988, entitled *Alicia: My Story*. It was translated into six languages, and Alicia became a sought-after speaker and activist. She passed away in April 2017, a month shy of her eighty-seventh birthday. Thousands of Jews survived the Holocaust with stories, such as Alicia's, and we are fortunate that so many have shared their experiences with us.

Chapter 6

Resistance, Luck, and the End of the War

After their success in the 1930s at expanding Germany and eradicating everyone they considered non-German, the Nazis were not prepared for the failures that awaited them in the following decade. On June 22, 1941, German troops invaded the Soviet Union in a maneuver Hitler called Operation Barbarossa. This endeavor was supposed to subdue the Soviets in a matter of months, if not weeks, yet it failed miserably.

At first, it seemed as though the Nazis would be successful, as Soviet defenses crumbled under the fierce Nazi onslaught, but the Soviet Army never stopped fighting back. In time, the limitation of Hitler's blitzkrieg began to show. It was meant to be a short, decisive effort, and was not suited to long, drawn-out warfare. The Nazis soon began to run short of troops, weaponry, and supplies, and they were not properly equipped to continue fighting the Soviet soldiers. Despite these setbacks, Hitler was adamant that they continue their efforts of murdering all Jews and other enemies of the Nazi Party throughout Europe.

A Soviet soldier feeds a child in a recently liberated village in June 1942.

Even as German troops struggled on the battlefield, Nazis further inside German borders continued to enact the murder of as many Jews as possible, and the trains to the death camps kept running. Day and night, the trains transported Jews from ghettos to killing centers with gas chambers and huge brick ovens—crematoria—to burn the bodies. Yet the resistance was only beginning.

The FPO

On New Year's Eve 1941, about 150 young activists gathered in the Vilna (Lithuania) ghetto. Any large gathering of Jews was likely to trigger Nazi suspicion, so they disguised the meeting as a New Year's Eve party. Their real purpose was to unite different youth groups into a fighting force. Abba Kovner, one of the most militant leaders in the Vilna ghetto, delivered an impassioned call to revolt:

> Let us not go like sheep to the slaughter, Jewish youth! Do not believe those who are deceiving you. Out of 80,000 Jews of the Jerusalem of Lithuania (Vilna), only 20,000 remain. In front of your eyes our parents, our brothers and our sisters are being torn away from us. Where are the hundreds of men who were snatched away for labor by the Lithuanian kidnappers? Where are those naked women who were taken away on the horror-night of the provocation? Where are those Jews of the Day of Atonement? And where are our brothers of the second ghetto? Anyone who is taken out through the gates of the ghetto, will never return. All roads of the ghetto lead to Ponary [a killing field outside of Vilna], and Ponary means death. Oh, despairing people—tear this deception away from your eyes. Your children, your husbands, your wives—are no longer alive— Ponary is not a labor camp. Everyone there is shot. Hitler aimed at destroying the Jews of Europe. It turned out to be the fate of the Jews of Lithuania to be the first. Let us not go like sheep to the slaughter. It is true that we are weak, lacking protection, but the only reply to a murderer is resistance. Brothers, it is better to die as free fighters than to live at the mercy of killers. Resist, resist, to our last breath.[1]

The reading had its intended effect. On the eve of 1942, Abba Kovner laid the foundation for what would become the United Partisans Organization or FPO (the Lithuanian initials). On September 1, 1943, the FPO attacked German troops who had come into the ghetto to seize two thousand

In 1961, Abba Kovner stands witness at the trial of Adolf Eichmann, a Nazi and SS leader.

Other Methods of Resistance

Armed defiance was not the only way of fighting back. Jews who could not take up arms found other ways to defy the Nazis. Young children risked their lives smuggling food to starving people in the ghettos. Jews of all ages ignored Nazi directives to keep their traditions alive: rabbis gathered people for Sabbath services; teachers held classes in bunkers and basements; diarists, historians, and social commentators recorded their experiences for posterity. Jews from all walks of life created hiding places, made daring escapes, and took life-or-death risks in the struggle for survival.

Jews. The partisans attacked but the ghetto leadership did not stand behind them. Abba Kovner realized that fighting inside the ghetto would be useless, so the partisans escaped through the sewers and established a base of operation in the Rudnicki forest. From there, they committed many acts of sabotage against German forces.

Escaping the Death Train

Eva Galler was seventeen when the Nazis began rounding up Jews in the ghetto of Lubaczow, Poland:

> Beginning on January 4, 1943, the Gestapo and the Polish and Ukrainian police started to chase all the Jews out from their houses. The deportation took several days. People ran and hid. The Jewish police helped to find the people in hiding. They had been promised that they would stay alive if they cooperated.

We knew where we were going. A boy from our town had been deported to Belzec camp. He escaped and came back to our town. He told us that Belzec had a crematorium. Deportation trains from other cities had passed by our city and people had thrown out notes. These notes were picked up by the men forced to work there. The notes said, "Don't take anything with you, just water."

They took us to a cattle train. People started to run away from the train, but they were shot. Once on the train we had to stand because there was no room to sit down. A boy tore the barbed wires from the train window. The young people started to jump out of the window. Many jumped. The SS on the rooftop of the train shot at them with rifles. My father told us, the oldest three, "Run, run—maybe you will stay alive. We will stay here with the small children because even if they get out, they will not be able to survive." . . .

My brother Berele jumped out, then my sister Hannah, and then I jumped out. The SS men shot at us. I landed in a snowbank. The bullets did not hit me. When I did not hear anything anymore, I went back to find my brother and my sister. I found them dead. My brother Berele was 15. My sister Hannah was 16. I was 17.[2]

The next day, Eva made her way through the woods to the train station in the city of Jaroslaw:

At that time it was thought that there were partisans in the woods. People were afraid to go in the woods, but I was not afraid. I was walking in the deep snow, and in the evening I came to the station. . . .

I bought a ticket for Cracow. I figured that Cracow was a big city with a big Jewish community. Maybe the

Jewish children on a tram car in the Warsaw ghetto. The Star of David on the front of the tram signifies that it can be used by Jews.

ghetto would still be there. In the train station I saw [someone I knew]... I was frightened that she might recognize me. I kept walking around the block until the train came.

Then I got on the train. This was another situation. I did not have any documents. . . . There were identification checks on the train. Every station I would move to another wagon.

In Cracow I spent two days and two nights living in the train station. There was a curfew at night because of the war. People who came into the city late had to stay in the train station until morning, so there were always a lot of people there. I moved around a lot so people would not recognize me, from one bench to another, from one room to another. It was a big station. But I did not have any money, and I did not have any bread. I had never been to Cracow before. . . . I did not see anybody with an armband, and I was scared to ask someone where the ghetto was.

I walked and walked. I was hungry. . . . I came to a market place, a farmers' market. I could hear running. They closed up the market place and took all the young people aside. I could hear the girls and boys talking. They were catching boys and girls and sending them to work in Germany. Nobody would go work freely in Germany; they had to use force. This was how they rounded up the people. I was very glad that I was caught with those people. I was caught as a Gentile and not as a Jew. . . . I assumed the identity of a Polish girl, Katarzyna Czuchowska, a name I made up.[3]

As Katarzyna, Eva survived the war years working on a farm in Austria.

Fighting in the Warsaw Ghetto

Meanwhile, conditions in Poland grew increasingly more difficult as the war raged on, and many Polish Jews began to consider military action. Jewish leaders in the Warsaw ghetto had initially rejected the idea of fighting back because they didn't take Nazi threats of deportation seriously. Yet Jewish teenagers and young adults began to band together in anticipation of deportations to come. Eventually, they formed the Jewish Fighting Organization, or ZOB (an acronym composed of its Polish initials).

In 1942 the ZOB officially became part of the Armia Krajowa, a Polish resistance movement founded earlier that year. They fought a limited action battle against the Nazis in January 1943, perhaps forcing the Nazis to regroup. About three months later, the Nazis came in force, and the fighters faced a battle they could neither delay nor win: when German troops came to destroy the ghetto and everyone in it, on April 19, 1943.

The ZOB had been preparing for this moment. Instead of allowing the Nazis to control them, they fought back with pistols, rifles, and homemade bombs. For nearly a month, they held off destruction and inflicted significant losses on the enemy. The battle ended with the ghetto in flames. A few survivors escaped to the non-Jewish side of the city, while others became trapped in underground bunkers within the still-burning ghetto.

Simha Rotem's father never allowed him to go to the Soviets, so he came of age in the Warsaw ghetto. In 1942, at age 17, he joined became a courier for the ZOB. He was given the code name Kazik and in 1943, after the April

102

The ZOB

The Żydowska Organizacja Bojowa (ZOB), or Jewish Fighting Organization, was a resistance group that formed in Poland after the Gross Aktion Warschau, the primary Aktion of the Warsaw ghetto. An Aktion was a major operation in which all of the Jews in a ghetto were collected and sent either to labor camps or to their deaths, and the beginnings of the Aktion in Warsaw made people living in the ghetto realize that resisting was a matter of life and death. Many secret organizations sprang up, but the ZOB was the largest. It was also made up mostly of young people, as youth groups had been suspicious of Nazi activity for a long time before the Aktion began. The ZOB supported armed resistance and was led by a twenty-three-year old named Mordecai Anielewicz. In 1942, the ZOB officially became part of the primary resistance movement in Poland, the Armia Krajowa (AK), and the AK began to supply the group with weapons. Using these weapons, the ZOB fought waves of Nazi deportations and led the Warsaw ghetto uprising in 1943, when the ghetto was finally destroyed.

Polish president Andrzej Duda pays his respects to the Ghetto Heroes Monument in Warsaw on the seventy-third anniversary of the Warsaw Ghetto Uprising in 2016.

uprising, participated in the ZOB attempt to rescue fighters who had been trapped in the fire-ravaged ghetto:

> After eleven or twelve days of battle . . . the Germans continued destroying the Ghetto from outside, with artillery bombardments and air attacks; finally, sappers [explosives experts] were sent to set fires and explode every cellar and bunker. In this situation . . . it was only a question of time until we would all be buried alive under the debris. The command staff therefore decided to find a way to rescue the fighters who could still be saved so they could continue fighting the Germans under other conditions.[4]

The partisans decided to go through the elaborate sewer system beneath the streets of Warsaw. Gradually a plan to get the fighters out of the ghetto took shape. "We needed an exit base where we could descend into the sewers; a guide from the sewer workers; and transportation to take the fighters . . . to the forest, where they would join a group of comrades who had left the Ghetto . . . and had been living in the forest since the end of April."[5]

The partisan escape through the sewers of Warsaw has become an enduring image of courage in the face of impossible odds. This was not the case immediately after the war as Simha Rotem discovered when he immigrated to Palestine (present-day Israel):

> A harsh and disappointing reality awaited me [there].
>
> My meeting with Melekh Neustadt, one of the first people I met here, concerned the fighters of the Warsaw Ghetto. I was interrogated about everyone who had been killed, but I was never asked, even remotely, about those who had survived.

> In almost every meeting with people in Eretz Israel, the question came up, "How did you survive?" It was asked again and again, and not always in the most delicate way. I had the feeling that I was guilty for surviving. This was why, even after I learned Hebrew, I didn't talk very much. . . . I preferred not to tell about myself and where I had spent the war years.[6]

Survivor guilt was common among Jews who survived while six million other Jews had perished. Probing questions only made matters worse. Rather than deal with them, many young survivors became reluctant to talk about their wartime experiences.

As the truth emerged through newsreels, photographs, diaries, and eyewitness accounts, a stunned world began to realize that the unthinkable was true: the ghettos, the killing fields, the cattle cars, the death camps, the six million Jewish victims and the millions of other victims— all of it, and many young survivors began to come forward with their stories.

The End of the War

By the spring of 1945, Hitler could no longer doubt that Germany was losing the war. The Soviets were closing from the east and the British and Americans from the west. In a desperate attempt to escape the Allies, guards at many camps rounded up prisoners who could still walk and fled with them toward the interior of Germany. These became known as death marches. As many as 15,000 Jews died on the march from Auschwitz.[7] Yet even before the marches started, sixteen-year-old Fritzie Weiss and fellow prisoners at Auschwitz sensed that the war was coming to an end:

Survivors of Auschwitz-Birkenau after the camp was liberated in 1945

[W]e knew because of the bombings and we knew because of the way the German soldiers were pushing us and pulling us already and emptying the camps. . . . They took us all and put us together, all of the people from camps, and they had us march through towns and through fields. They didn't know where to put us anymore and they didn't know what to do with us and there was no food because the Germans were losing the war. Oftentimes as they marched us through a town, a window would open and a shutter would open and either a potato or a loaf of bread would come flying out and the shutter would close after. And we would all pounce on this potato or . . . whatever this piece of food was that came at us. And of course [the guards] would shoot at us, but we didn't care at that point because we were hungry. The streets were literally covered with bodies as we marched. We would pass . . . body after body after body, people that were dropping dead from hunger, from disease, from dysentery, because they did not have the strength or because they gave up.[8]

The Holocaust took away Sam Itzkowitz's youth. He was fourteen when the war started and twenty when it ended. Sam was in Dachau when the guards and staff rounded up prisoners and marched them toward the Bavarian Alps:

Till today I don't know what the reason was. Either they wanted to destroy us . . . in those mountains or they were going to trade us off through Switzerland. There was the death march. Well, I was already so weak that I could barely walk. That march . . . took about . . . ten days to two weeks. Snow in the daytime, snow at night . . And we had to sleep outside . . . they always camped us out somewhere in an open field. And we just huddled together like animals . . . in the wilderness. And tried to, just tried to stay alive. And on top of it, we saw planes coming over us . . . And we were praying, hoping . . . "Come on, drop them, get it over with." Well I don't know. I think the pilots saw that we were prisoners and they dropped bombs all around us, but never on us. See we were wearing those striped . . . uniforms. And they didn't fly too high to start with because they were bombing in the daytime. So probably this is the only thing that saved us.[9]

Luck and Survival

The idea of luck appears often in survivor testimony, like that of Sam Itkowitz. Survivors made it clear that they were not smarter, more courageous, or more deserving than those who died. They just happened to run away in the nick of time, find helpers when they needed them most, or were out of reach when the Nazis were filling the death camps.

Decades after surviving the war as a teenager, Alexander Schenker encapsulated this sense of luck as a driving factor:

> I am convinced now that in life everything is a question of luck. We were immensely lucky in all kinds of ways throughout the war. I mean considering the place where we found ourselves, and that is at the very [center] . . . of this horror, to get out of it in the shape in which we got out of it took an immense amount of luck. And . . . you know luck is really a question of coincidence. You happen . . . to turn left when you have a choice to go straight and to go right. You don't know . . . why you are going left, and yet to turn left turns out to be the lucky [choice].[10]

The Right Place and the Right Time

Ten-year-old Thomas Buergenthal had his own definition of luck—it was anything that kept him alive, however terrible the event itself might be. By that standard, losing several toes to frostbite in the brutal winter of 1945 was a stroke of luck. Thomas was laid up at Sachsenhausen (a camp near Berlin) when the Germans decided to run. On April 21, 1945, they grabbed every prisoner who could still walk and fled toward the mountains. Thomas was among the prisoners left behind in the so-called hospital ward. This was actually the last stop before the gas chambers.

When the Germans fled they did not have time to use the gas, so the hospital inmates expected to be shot in their beds. Decades later, Thomas recalled that fateful day:

> I remember . . . when people lined up, and then it became extremely quiet, and you couldn't hear anything. . . . And we waited, basically on the assumption that any minute now [the Germans] would come in. Nothing happened. . . . I had a crutch and I could move. . . . [So] I went out to look, because [of] all this silence. And . . . the camp was empty . . . the Germans had left. . . . By then, you could hear already the rumbling of artillery . . . in the background. And there wasn't a soul to be seen. . . . Eventually . . . the gates swung open, and . . . Russian troops came in. And they began ringing . . . the camp bell to say that we were free.[11]

The Soviets came into camp on April 22, just one day after the Germans left. The prisoners on the death march were not rescued for another thirteen days; time enough for hundreds more to die. Thomas might well have been among them.

Thomas did not feel guilty for his near-miraculous survival, though he knew survivors who carried a burden of guilt because they had lived while so many others did not:

> I have never experienced these [guilt] feelings. I don't know why, but if I were to speculate, I would attribute their absence to the instinctive belief of children in their own immortality and their entitlement to live. It may also be that since I attributed my survival to sheer luck, I came to view survival and non- survival as a game of chance over which I had no control and was, therefore, not responsible for the outcome.[12]

Regardless of how they lived through the Holocaust, young survivors faced hard times after the war. Thousands had no place to go and no one to care for them. The Nazis had destroyed their homes and killed their families After enduring the unthinkable, they had to muster the courage for yet another task—figuring out how to build a future despite the trauma that marred their pasts. The stories they carried from the center of the Holocaust remind us of the terrible evil humans are capable of, while their lives beyond that terrible time serve as examples of the resilience of the human spirit.

1938

July 6–15—Evian Conference on German-Jewish refugees.

November 9–10—Kristallnacht; mass violence and vandalism against Jews in Germany.

December 1–September 1, 1939—Kindertransport program takes many Jewish children to safety in England.

1939

May 13–June 17—Voyage of the SS *St. Louis* from Europe to Cuba and back again.

September 1—Germany invades Poland.

September 27—Warsaw surrenders to Germany.

1940

April 9—Germany invades Denmark and Norway.

May 10—Germany invades Holland, Belgium, and France.

October 12—Warsaw ghetto established.

November 16—Warsaw ghetto sealed off;
Jews not allowed to leave.

1941

June 22—Germany invades Soviet Union; Einsatzgruppen death squads begin wholesale slaughter of Jews.

1942

January 20—Wannsee conference coordinates the "final solution to the Jewish question."

January 21—The resistance organization FPO is formed in Vilna, Lithuania.

1943

April 19–May 16—Warsaw ghetto uprising.

June 21—SS orders complete destruction of all ghettos in Poland.

1944

March 19—Germany invades Hungary and begins deporting Jews to camps.

1945

January—Allies advance on German positions; death marches begin.

April 30—Hitler commites suicide in his bunker.

May 8—Germany surrenders unconditionally to the Allies.

Introduction

1. United States Holocaust Memorial Museum, "Documenting Numbers of Victims oft the Holocaust and Nazi Persecution," Holocaust Encyclopedia, n.d., <https://www.ushmm.org/wlc/en/article.php?ModuleId=10008193> (accessed on October 9, 2017).

Chapter 1
Choosing When to Flee

1. United States Holocaust Memorial Museum, "Nuremberg Laws," *Holocaust Encyclopedia,* https://www.ushmm.org/wlc/en/article.php?ModuleId=10007902.
2. Liane Reif-Lehrer, *Oral History Interview*, United States Holocaust Memorial Museum (USHMM) Archives, RG-50.233*0108.
3. "Kristallnacht Order: November 10, 1938," Jewish Virtual Library, 2017, http://www.jewishvirtuallibrary.org/kristallnacht-order.
4. "Kristallnacht: Background and Overview," Jewish Virtual Library, 2009, http://www.jewishvirtuallibrary.org/background-and-overview-of-kristallnacht.
5. Fred Ederer, *Survivor Testimonies*, USHMM Archives, RG-01.087.
6. Gerda Feldman, *Oral History*, USHMM Archives, RG-50.030*0429.
7. Kazik (Simha Rotem), *Memoirs of a Warsaw Ghetto Fighter* (New Haven, CT: Yale University Press. 1994), p. 10.
8. Yitzhak Zuckerman, *A Surplus of Memory: Chronicle of the Warsaw Ghetto Uprising* (Berkeley, CA: University of California Press, 1993), p. 3.
9. United States Holocaust Museum, "Lebensraum," Holocaust Encyclopedia, https://www.ushmm.org/wlc/en/article.php?ModuleId=10008219.

10. Charlene Schiff (Shulamit Perlmutter), "The Haystack—1942," USHMM, 2002, https://www.ushmm.org/remember/office-of-survivor-affairs/memory-project/featured-writers/schiff-haystack.

Chapter 2
Traveling Through Hostile Territory

1. Ursula Bacon, *Shanghai Diary: A Young Girl's Journey from Hitler's Hate to War-Torn China* (Milwaukie, OR: M Press, 2004), pp. 13–14
2. Ibid., p. 13.
3. "Leo Melamed: Family Odyssey," United States Holocaust Memorial Museum: Flight and Rescue, https://www.ushmm.org/exhibition/flight-rescue/vid_player.php?id=2771.
4. Ibid.
5. Ibid.
6. Eva Rappoport Edmands, "Describes Packing to Leave Vienna for France in 1938," Personal Histories: Refugees, United States Holocaust Memorial Museum, https://www.ushmm.org/exhibition/personal-history/media_oi.php?MediaId=2893.
7. Edith Schleissner Nathan, "A Survivor from Czechoslovakia," Hunter College H.S. Holocaust Survivors, http://shatteredcrystals.net/hchs/hchs_accounts2.htm.
8. Ibid.
9. Ibid.
10. Ibid.
11. Evelyn Konrad, "Dodging U-boats Crossing the Atlantic," Hunter College H.S. Holocaust Survivors, http://shatteredcrystals.net/hchs/hchs_accounts6.htm.
12. Ibid.
13. Lucille Szepsenwol Camhi, "Family Odyssey," USHMM online exhibit, https://www.ushmm.org/exhibition/flight-rescue/vid_player.php?id=2768.
14. Ibid.

15. United States Holocaust Memorial Museum. "Chiune (Sempo) Sugihara." *Holocaust Encyclopedia,* https://www.ushmm.org/wlc/en/article.php?ModuleId=10005594.
16. Lucille Szepsenwol Camhi, "Family Odyssey," USHMM online exhibit, https://www.ushmm.org/exhibition/flight-rescue/vid_player.php?id=2768.

Chapter 3
The Kindertransport and the *St. Louis*

1. Norbert Wollheim, "Kindertransport. 1938–1940," USHMM, https://www.ushmm.org/wlc/en/media_oi.php?ModuleId=10005260&MediaId=2489.
2. Alice Eberstarkova Masters, *Oral History Transcript*, United States Holocaust Memorial Museum (USHMM) Archives, RG-50.030*0360.
3. Ibid.
4. Alice Eberstarkova Masters, "Kindertransport. 1938–1940," USHMM, https://www.ushmm.org/wlc/en/media_oi.php?ModuleId=0&MediaId=2479.
5. Ibid.
6. National Institute of Mental Health. "Post-Traumatic Stress Disorder," https://www.nimh.nih.gov/health/topics/post-traumatic-stress-disorder-ptsd/index.shtml.
7. Bessel Van der Kolk, "Posttraumatic Stress Disorder and Memory." *Psychiatric Times*, http://www.psychiatrictimes.com/ptsd/posttraumatic-stress-disorder-and-memory.
8. Inge Sachs Rosenthal, *Oral History Interview*, USHMM Archives, RG-50.030*0389.
9. Ibid.
10. Gerda Blachmann Wilchfort, *Oral History Interview*, USHMM Archives, RG-50.030*0251.
11. Gerda Feldman, *Oral History*, USHMM Archives, RG-50.030*0429.
12. Blachmann Wilchfort.
13. Feldman.

Chapter 4
Life on the Run

1. Alfred Feldman and Susan Zuccotti, *One Step Ahead: A Jewish Fugitive in Hitler's Europe* (Carbondale, IL: Southern Illinois University Press), pp. 97–98.

2. Ibid., p. 102.

3. Ibid., p. 101.

4. United States Holocaust Memorial Museum, "Einsatzgruppen (Mobile Killing Units)," *Holocaust Encyclopedia,* https://www.ushmm.org/wlc/en/article.php?ModuleId=10005130.

5. Sally Eisner, "Personal Reflections—In Hiding," Women and the Holocaust, https://www.fold3.com/page/285875802_holocaust_survivors_their_stories/stories.

6. Ibid.

7. Florence Gittelman Eisen, *Oral History Interview*, United States Holocaust Memorial Museum (USHMM) Archives, RG-50.030*0260.

8. Margrit Rosenberg Stenge, "Margrit's Story: Narrow Escape to and from Norway," the Concordia University Chair in Canadian Jewish Studies and the Montreal Institute for Genocide and Human Rights Studies, 2004, http://migs.concordia.ca/memoirs/margit_rosenberg_stenge/margrit_rosenberg_stenge_02.htm.

9. Ibid.

10. Evelyn Konrad, "Dodging U-boats Crossing the Atlantic," Hunter College H.S. Holocaust Survivors, http://shatteredcrystals.net/er.kugler/hchs/hchs_accounts6.htm.

11. Ibid.

12. Hanni Sondheimer Vogelweid, "Flight and Rescue," USHMM, https://www.ushmm.org/exhibition/flight-rescue/vid_player.php?id=2770.

13. Ibid.

14. Ruth Berkowicz Segal, "Polish Jews in Lithuania: Escape to Japan ," USHMM, https://www.ushmm.org/wlc/en/media_oi.php?ModuleId=10005588&MediaId=5257.

15. Johanna Gerechter Neumann, "Survivor Volunteers," USHMM, https://www.ushmm.org/remember/

office-of-survivor-affairs/survivor-volunteer/johanna-gerechter-neumann.

16. Erika Eckstut (Neuman), "Lasting Memory," USHMM, https://www.ushmm.org/remember/office-of-survivor-affairs/memory-project/featured-writers/eckstut-memory.

17. Rosa Weintraub, "Memoirs of Roza Weintraub—Her Oral History Prepared at Kibbutz Nir David—26.6.1985," https://kehilalinks.jewishgen.org/kibart/rozamem.html.

Chapter 5
Alicia's Journey

1. Alicia Appleman-Jurman, *Alicia: My Story* (New York, NY: Bantam Books, 1989), p. 13.
2. Ibid., p. 95.
3. Ibid., p. 139.
4. Ibid., p. 174.
5. Ibid., p. 180.
6. Ibid., p. 181.

Chapter 6
Resistance, Luck, and the End of the War

1. Abba Kovner, "The First Call: Manifesto of Jewish Resistance by Abba Kovner," Holocaust Survivors.org, http://www.holocaustsurvivors.org/data.show.php?di=record&da=texts&ke=1.
2. "Survivor Stories: Eva Galler," Holocaust Survivors, http://www.holocaustsurvivors.org/data.show.php?di=record&da=survivors&ke=6.
3. Ibid.
4. Kazik (Simha Rotem), *Memoirs of a Warsaw Ghetto Fighter* (New Haven, CT: Yale University Press, 1994), p. 41.
5. Ibid., p. 49.
6. Ibid., pp. 152–153.
7. "Auschwitz," United States Holocaust Memorial Museum (USHMM), May 4, 2009, http://www.ushmm.org/wlc/article.php?ModuleId= 10005189.

8. Fritzie Weiss Fritzshall, "Describes the Death March from Auschwitz," United States Holocaust Memorial Museum (USHMM), https://www.ushmm.org/outreach/en/media_oi.php?MediaId=2863.

9. Sam Itzkowitz, "Describes a Death March from Landsberg, a Subcamp of Dachau, to the Bavarian Alps," USHMM, https://www.ushmm.org/wlc/en/media_oi.php?ModuleId=0&MediaId=1216.

10. Alexander Schenker, "Describes How He Is Convinced Now That in Life Everything Is a Question of Luck," USHMM, https://www.ushmm.org/exhibition/flight-rescue/vid_player.php?id=2707.

11. Thomas Buergenthal, "Describes the Liberation of the Sachsenhausen Camp," 1990 Interview, USHMM, https://www.ushmm.org/outreach/en/media_oi.php?MediaId=2611.

12. Thomas Buergenthal, *A Lucky Child: A Memoir of Surviving Auschwitz as a Young Boy* (New York, NY: Little, Brown and Company, 2009), p. 209.

Glossary

Aktion German word for "action." A raid in which Jews in ghettos were rounded up and sent to work camps or death camps.

annex To take possession of territory through seizure or conquest.

anti-Semitism Fear and hatred of Jews.

Aryan Originally, people speaking certain languages. The Nazis used the term to denote what they called a race of people of Germanic background who were, typically, tall, blond, and blue-eyed.

bigotry Lack of tolerance toward those who have different ideas and faiths.

blitzkrieg Literally "lightning war" (German). A form of warfare that used short, rapid attacks to break through enemy defenses by overwhelming them.

Brownshirts Members of the Sturmabteilung (SA), the Nazi private police force. Also called stormtroopers. The SA was largely replaced by the SS in 1934.

bunker An underground fortification or hiding place.

chancellor Head of state in a parliamentary government.

concentration camp A prison for civilians, political prisoners, and enemy aliens, including Jews.

death camp A facility designed for mass murder, with gas chambers and crematory ovens.

death march Forced evacuation of Jewish prisoners by Germans fleeing Allied troops.

Einsatzgruppen German killing squads that operated in the Soviet Union after the German invasion in June 1941.

emigrate To leave one country and settle in another.

fascism A form of government based on nationalism and power held by a single individual or small group.

final solution The term for the Nazi plan to solve what they called the "Jewish problem" or "Jewish question" by killing all the Jews in Europe.

Gentile A non-Jewish person.

Gestapo (Geheimestaatspolizei) Internal security police known for terrorist methods against persons suspected of treason or disloyalty to Nazi Germany.

ghetto A part of a city, usually viewed as undesirable, where minority groups are isolated.

interrogate To question officially and often intensively.

partisans Fighting units of people who organized themselves like army units.

propaganda Speech, writing, or other form of communication aimed at persuading people to think or believe a certain way.

refugee A person who has been forced to cross national borders because they are unsafe in their home country.

Schutzstaffel (SS) Military-like organization. Members of the SS served as camp guards and police.

xenophobia Irrational fear of people from other countries or ethnicities.

Further Reading

Books

Appleman-Jurman, Alicia. *Alicia: Memoirs of a Survivor*. New York, NY: Bantam, 2014.

Arata, Rona. *The Ship to Nowhere*. Toronto, ON: Second Story Press, 2016.

Engle, Margarita. *Tropical Secrets: Holocaust Refugees in Cuba*. New York, NY: Square Fish, 2009.

Gillette, Robert H. *Escape to Virginia: From Nazi Germany to Thalhimer S Farm*. Mount Pleasant, SC: Arcadia Publishing, 2016.

Gold, Alison Leslie. *A Special Fate: Chiune Sugihara: Hero of the Holocaust*. New York, NY: Scholastic 2014.

Shackleton, Kath. *Survivors of the Holocaust*. London, UK: Hachette: 2016.

Websites

BBC – The Holocaust Year by Year
www.bbc.co.uk/timelines/z86nfg8
> *An interactive timeline displaying the events of each year of the Holocaust.*

History Channel Online
www.history.com/topics/world-war-ii/the-holocaust
> *The online branch of the History Channel offers videos and articles about the Holocaust more generally.*

How Stuff Works: Stuff You Missed in History Class
www.missedinhistory.com/tags/world-war-ii.htm
> *A plethora of podcasts on all aspects of World War II.*

The United States Holocaust Memorial Museum
www.ushmm.org/learn/students/the-holocaust-a-learning-site-for-students
> *The museum, located in Washington, DC, has a vast online archive of survivor interviews, informational articles, videos, and images.*

Films

Defiance, dir. Edward Zwick, 2008.

"Escape from Auschwitz," April 29, 2008, *Secrets of the Dead: Unearthing History*, PBS, television program.